A Balanced Epistemological Orientation for the Social Sciences

A Balanced Epistemological Orientation for the Social Sciences

Charles F. Gattone

LEXINGTON BOOKS

Lanham • Boulder • New York • London

Published by Lexington Books
An imprint of The Rowman & Littlefield Publishing Group, Inc.
4501 Forbes Boulevard, Suite 200, Lanham, Maryland 20706
www.rowman.com

6 Tinworth Street, London SE11 5AL, United Kingdom

British Library Cataloguing in Publication Information Available

Library of Congress Cataloging-in-Publication Data Available

ISBN 978-1-7936-3144-2 (cloth)
ISBN 978-1-7936-3146-6 (paper)
ISBN 978-1-7936-3145-9 (electronic)

For Lizzie, Max, and Angela Rose

Contents

Introduction

Given the abundance of classical and contemporary writing on the theoretical issues involved in social research, it seems odd that so many social scientists continue to operate as though they are not familiar with these discussions. Some scholars have gone as far as to suggest that it is possible to engage in research in the absence of theory altogether and focus only on the empirical facts involved. This has fostered a situation where a growing range of social scientific work lacks a solid conceptual foundation and is unable to withstand the critique of the theoretically informed social thinker.

To be fair, we should acknowledge that social theory has been suffering from a bit of confusion in its domain as well. Theory has undergone several major transformations over the course of its history and broken apart into a number of competing perspectives, each with its own set of starting assumptions, mode of logic, and criticisms of alternative views. While this diversity can be seen as a strength, it leaves researchers at a loss in their effort to integrate theory into their work. Theorists have also been known to employ their own rather specialized language that is difficult to understand from the non-theorist's point of view, and this further contributes to the confusion of researchers trying to make sense of it and use it in their investigations.

The rift between theory and research also grows as social scientists uncritically adopt perspectives and methods that are commonly used in their respective fields. This practice carries older, entrenched ideas forward from one generation of scholars to the next and diminishes the potential for innovative thinking on the issues involved. Theory in this environment becomes a mundane requirement for investigators to include in their work and an additional burden in the larger process of constructing and completing a viable research project.

One concern in this regard centers on the area of social theory that involves thinking about knowledge itself and, in particular, about the process of developing new knowledge of the social world. Researchers generally seek to construct insightful assessments of social phenomena, but they often engage in inquiry without being fully aware of the ways their own perceptions may be limiting their investigations. Social scientists approach their research in relation to a specific set of cultural norms and traditions, and these can have a significant bearing on the directions of their inquiry, from shaping their choices about what to study to the analyses they develop. This leads us to the important point that there is no escaping the influence of perspective in social research.

This issue in itself would be of minor concern if social scientists recognized this influence and consciously approached their work in this light, but the reality is that they often fail to acknowledge this dimension of social research and instead follow a course of action that resonates with the established practices of their individual disciplines. Their inclination, in this sense, is to operate from the standpoint of one of the conventionally accepted epistemological orientations in their field and overlook the impact of this choice on their conclusions.

In light of this state of affairs, it seems worthwhile to establish a balanced epistemological orientation for researchers to rely on in their investigations. Doing so involves drawing on the strengths of existing orientations in the field to reveal how they have contributed to social research, as well as how they have fallen short in certain respects. It means tempering these ideas with an awareness of the practical challenges facing social scientists and thinking about how these may be interfering with their potential to incorporate some of the more subtle contributions of social theory into their analyses. The goal of this book is thus to identify an epistemological orientation for the social sciences that provides a theoretically informed conceptual foundation for innovative and insightful research.

This project begins with a critical examination of four salient epistemological orientations in the social sciences: positivism, relativism, interpretivism, and intersubjectivism.[1] It highlights their strengths, but also reveals how each falters in terms of its ability to singlehandedly serve as a guide for social research. Rather than discounting these four entirely, we draw on what they have to offer and introduce additional considerations to strike a balance between their various contributions. The purpose of this effort is not to simply tear down these orientations, but to help researchers confront these issues and hopefully enhance the quality of their work on the whole.[2]

This may be the appropriate place to mention that this book is not intended to diminish or in any manner undermine the legitimacy of the epistemological orientations of the natural sciences. It is understood that these are valuable and have proven to be very helpful as a way to learn about the natural world. This book does not call these into question, but embraces the point of view that the social sciences exhibit some differences from their natural counterparts and that the unique nature of the former requires the construction of an epistemological orientation capable of standing on its own. The aim is thus to identify the characteristics of an epistemological orientation that does not simply emulate those of the natural sciences but reflects the distinctive qualities of social science and provides the conceptual foundation needed to reach its full potential. There is certainly some overlap in terms of the work of these two broadly defined areas of inquiry; however, their differences are sufficient to warrant the need for an epistemological orientation that is specifically tailored to social science. Combining the two together as one and assuming that their respective endeavors are identical is part of the problem facing the social sciences in the present context. Developing an awareness of the distinctive features of social science and clarifying how to think about this kind of work is a central goal of this project.

The first chapter of the book outlines the ideas of positivism and its practices. It begins by identifying the main assumptions, logic, and goals of this orientation and offers an assessment of its influence in the social sciences. Positivism has both helped and hindered social research in that it has given rise to findings that are able to withstand critical scrutiny while also narrowing the scope of research projects and pulling investigators away from studying some of the more subtle aspects of the social world. Most researchers have moved beyond the basics of positivism, but the spirit of this orientation continues to provide a strong undercurrent in the social sciences today.

Chapter 2 reviews the ideas associated with relativism and addresses the connections of these ideas to social inquiry. Relativism has drawn attention to the uncertainty of social science and expanded the range of perspectives in each field, but it has also displayed some internal contradictions, and these have created difficulties for scholars trying to rely on its conceptual positions in their work. These ideas have shaken the legitimacy of established convention and exposed some of the heretofore unaddressed contradictions of positivism, opening up the field to new avenues of inquiry. This influence cannot be overlooked when considering the concomitant weaknesses of relativism as an epistemological orientation.

Chapter 3 focuses on the fundamentals of interpretivism and its emphasis on some of the more personal ways of learning about people from their own point of view and in their own milieu. One of the main characteristics of this orientation is its focus on the meanings people bring to their behavior in everyday life. Researchers relying on this epistemological orientation provide insight into the interpersonal interactions of individuals and groups in a range of social settings. They are skilled at breaking down the barriers of misunderstanding that separate one culture from the next and at revealing the dynamics of previously hidden or poorly understood social worlds. This chapter shows that the ideas of interpretivism do not need to be limited to interpersonal research, but can be applied to large-scale investigations as well. In carving out a middle ground between positivism and relativism, interpretivism brings us closer to a balanced epistemological orientation for the social sciences.

Chapter 4 turns to a discussion of the intersubjective orientation and its relevance to social research. It begins with a review of its early contributors—Husserl, Schütz, Peirce, James, and Dewey—and then moves on to the ideas of Habermas and his critique of the positivist and relativist orientations. Habermas and others in the intersubjectivist camp have stated quite clearly that while the positivist approach to social research does have epistemological shortcomings, it is not necessary to conclude—as the relativists have done—that it is therefore doubtful that the social sciences have the potential to yield any degree of truth about the social world. Habermas emphasized the idea that the epistemological foundations of social science can be formed collectively through debate and discussion, where scholars develop assertions on the basis of mutually agreed-upon principles. Truth in this context is seen as provisional rather than absolute and may shift over time as new evidence and analyses emerge.

The intersubjective orientation offers a compelling alternative to the others, but it also possesses some stumbling blocks, and these are not adequately addressed by its purveyors. Issues of power, the inherent diversity of ideas, and the obstacles involved in working toward consensus do require additional discussion, but these issues do not undermine the theoretical rigor of intersubjectivism on the whole. Its emphasis on the constructed dimensions of social scientific knowledge together with its proposed solution in the quest for mutual understanding provide a unique contribution to the effort to address these issues.

Chapter 5 brings these assessments together in an integrated fashion to identify the characteristics of a balanced epistemological orientation for the social sciences. A central argument of this chapter is that the interpretive nature of social science does not diminish its potential to reveal new insight into the social world. Social phenomena can, at times, be difficult to fully understand, but this ambiguity does not mean that one cannot make some headway toward this goal. While social scientists certainly face formidable obstacles to constructing solid analyses, research conducted in an epistemologically balanced, empirically grounded, and theoretically informed manner can significantly aid in this endeavor. The task of social inquiry is more than simply gathering factual information about social phenomena and passing it on to others. It involves constructing categories, making judgments about how to view social issues, creatively analyzing data to reach new conclusions, and communicating these findings to others. These steps cannot be taken in the absence of a conceptual framework.

The interpretive nature of social science is one of the reasons it has been such a contested space throughout human history. When researchers develop new ideas about their subject matter, they are unavoidably engaged in the ongoing struggle to define social reality. Their work requires that they take a stand and assert the validity of one set of frames over another. Social scientific analysis always relies on specific values, norms, and traditions, whether its practitioners realize this or not. The notion that social scientists are neutral observers gathering value-free information no longer carries much weight in the realm of social theory. It is crucial for researchers interested in improving the quality of their work to recognize this premise and reflect on it as they carry out their investigations and interpret their findings.

Social science is situated at the heart of some of the more important decisions taking place in contemporary society. Its main goals involve studying social reality in a cogent and meaningful manner and developing analyses that have a direct relevance to the present and future directions of civilization. Approaching social research from a balanced epistemological orientation means accepting the idea that, although this work is connected to a particular set of norms and traditions, it has the potential to produce enlightening assessments of social phenomena as they relate to people's everyday lives. Being aware of the epistemological challenges involved in social research and addressing these directly are essential prerequisites to intelligently and insightfully understanding today's dynamic and ever-changing social world.

NOTES

1. These four do not represent a comprehensive survey of all epistemological orientations in the field, but they are prevalent in the social sciences and each of these possesses characteristics worthy of consideration when putting together a balanced orientation.

2. The reader may notice in the text of this book that I use the term "orientation" when addressing epistemological matters and other terms such as "perspective" or "outlook" when discussing the theoretical framing of research projects. This is done in an effort to draw attention to the differences between these domains and to highlight the notion that it is possible for researchers operating on the basis of a particular epistemological orientation to have differing theoretical perspectives regarding their topic of study. Similarly, it is possible for researchers relying on different epistemological orientations to draw on the same or similar theoretical perspectives. Regarding the possibility of defining these terms in the abstract, I defer to the comments of Pierre Bourdieu, who argued that the "notorious operational definition" seeks to settle on

paper that which is not definitively settled in reality. Rather than attempting to sum-
marize the meanings of these terms apart from their usage, I employ an approach that
allows their meanings to come across as they appear in the text as a whole. This is to
say that reading this work and observing the use of these terms will hopefully provide
readers with a more accurate and in-depth understanding of their meanings than those
that could have been provided in a few sentences. For more on Bourdieu's position
on this, please see Pierre Bourdieu, "Thinking About Limits," *Theory, Culture, &
Society* 9 (1992): 37–49.

Chapter 1

Positivism

Cutting through the Myths

One of the central ironies of social theory is that while the term "positivism" has come to invoke a critical and generally negative reaction, the ideas behind this orientation continue to provide the foundation for the practices of social scientists today. While most scholars are at least somewhat aware of the problems of positivism, its underlying ethos still serves as the de facto starting point upon which much of the research and analysis around the world is based. It therefore seems worthwhile to take a moment to think about its strengths and weaknesses and consider its relevance both to the development of social scientific knowledge and to the domain of knowledge in general. Our goal, in this sense, is to try to identify aspects of positivism that are valuable and worth retaining as we work toward the formation of a balanced epistemological orientation for social science.

The primary aim of social research in the positivist tradition is to forge unbiased assessments of the areas of the social world one is studying. From this point of view, there is a reality that exists independently of human understanding, and the task of social research is to learn about that reality through investigation and analysis. One might characterize this endeavor as observing human social life under a magnifying glass to see it more clearly and share this newfound knowledge with others to help them understand it better as well.

A principal characteristic of positivism is the requirement that claims about the everyday world be supported by empirical evidence. Rather than giving credence to ideas that appear to be true on the basis of informal experience, the task of social research from within this orientation is to sift through any potential distortions that may be present in one analysis or another and discover the truth about the social reality being studied.

In addition to seeking new knowledge about the social world, a second goal of social science from the positivist orientation is to draw on this knowledge in order to make informed decisions. The broader aim of social research is to address complex matters in an enlightened way and enhance the quality of human existence generally. Rather than relying on speculation, conventional belief, or personal opinion, research done in the positivist tradition strives to develop an objective accounting of the social world which can then be used to improve the quality of decision-making at the personal and public levels.

AUGUSTE COMTE

We can trace the ideas of positivism to several early modern social thinkers, but the best known and most influential of these in the Western world was Auguste Comte, the founder of the positivist philosophy. Comte was a French philosopher living during the historical transition in Europe from the decline of feudalism to the early stages of industrial capitalism. He observed that the older aristocratic order had crumbled and left in its wake an entirely new but undefined form of societal organization. In his analysis, the French Revolution brought an end to the outmoded monarchical traditions in France, but also created a power vacuum that had yet to be filled. He argued that during the years after the revolution, the persistent conflict between competing political groups fostered a chaotic social environment that prevented France and much of Europe from establishing a new and more stable societal order.[1]

Comte acknowledged that the practical constraints placed on political and economic leaders played a significant role in perpetuating this instability, but he also believed that the ongoing chaos was due in large part to conceptual weaknesses in the world of ideas. He maintained that during the feudal era, the widespread belief that the king and queen held a direct connection to God provided the crucial footing upon which the authority of the aristocracy could rest. Decisions made by these leaders were seen as legitimate in this context due to a prevalent faith in divine right. Comte pointed out that this belief system significantly eroded with the collapse of the ancien régime and that no single philosophical orientation had arisen to take its place. He suggested that until a newer and equally effective philosophy emerged, disorder would continue to prevail and inhibit the advance of civilization in the future.[2]

The solution to this problem from Comte's point of view could be found in the domain of science and in particular in the development of a science of society. He believed that the positive philosophy and its application to the examination of the social world would eventually eliminate the misunderstandings that had persisted throughout human history, paving the way for a nascent form of societal organization grounded in scientific fact. He expected

social science to contribute to the formation of universal laws and characterized this new field of study as "social physics."[3] He expected this newfound
knowledge to then be applied to the management of the social order and help
bring an end to the turmoil associated with the lack of information and poor
judgment in the public sphere. Comte was an atheist, but he characterized
the realm of ideas as the "spiritual" and the realm of practical affairs as the
"temporal," identifying the problem in the following way:

> Spiritual anarchy has preceded and engendered temporal anarchy. In the pres-
> ent epoch the social malady depends much more on the first than on the second
> cause. On the other hand an attentive study of the progress of civilization proves
> that the spiritual is now more completely prepared than the temporal reorganiza-
> tion of society. Thus our first efforts to terminate the revolutionary epoch should
> aim at reorganizing the spiritual power.[4]

Comte believed that scientifically derived knowledge could be free of the
errors and misunderstandings that had plagued leaders in the past and that
the positivist philosophy would eventually provide a stable foundation for
decision-making in the newer order. Just as discoveries in the natural sciences had given rise to new ways to understand the physical world, so too
would the scientific investigation of society reveal new truths about the social
world.

Comte argued that studying the social world scientifically would clarify
the future directions of modern society by revealing the ongoing trends in
the recent past and observe their development into the present. This type
of knowledge would enable scholars to see where society was heading and
shed new light on the actions needed to guide it in the right direction. He
posited that social science would be capable of providing not only descriptive assessments of current phenomena but also prescriptive advice regarding the steps needed to help civilization advance into the future. His belief
was that the findings of social science would eventually be able to convey
the most prudent policies and thus serve in the best interest of humanity in
the long run.[5]

His faith in the predictive qualities of social science led Comte to proclaim
that this form of knowledge would enable political leaders to address not
only organizational matters but complex moral issues as well. He argued
that knowing the "natural" course of events as they were to unfold in the
future could guide social scientists toward what he characterized as the
"natural morality of man."[6] He maintained that this knowledge would inform
policymakers of the proper set of morals and provide a new foundation for
establishing norms and laws to enforce this morality for the sake of the public
good. He articulated his position in the following way:

> Hence the necessity for developing, by a special influence, the natural morality
> of man, in order, as much as possible, to bring the impulses of all within the
> limits required for the general harmony, by habituating them from childhood to
> a voluntary subordination of their personal interest to the common interest, and
> by constantly producing in active life, with necessary emphasis, the consider-
> ation of the social point of view.[7]

Comte sincerely believed that a science of society would be capable of providing the insight needed to make moral decisions and guide the formation of
public policy, both with regard to the larger directions of the social order and
in identifying the proper behavior of individuals living in this order. Social
science, from Comte's perspective, could thus unveil the new guiding principles that would take the place of divine right and set the modern world on
its proper and "natural" path. Political leaders and their respective institutions
in government would then be charged with the task of implementing these
findings through the systematic management of society. Comte called this a
"positive polity" where questions about norms, values, and morality could all
be answered through scientific study and directly linked to public policy as a
matter of course.[8]

Subsequent purveyors of the positivist orientation have not carried this
claim to moral authority forward in a literal fashion, but have retained the
idea that scientifically grounded knowledge about the social world can provide the basis for decision-making on a practical level.[9] This approach in
its more contemporary form draws on the goals outlined by Comte in the
sense that it operates according to the assumption that scientifically derived
knowledge about the social world is of a higher order than that constructed
in other ways, and that this type of knowledge is best able to inform scholars
and political leaders of the true nature of the ongoing events and trends in the
everyday world. The belief that social scientific conclusions can serve as a
guide for the practical management of public affairs continues to be an integral component of the positivist tradition and informs the logic of many social
scientists in the present. The goal of social research from this point of view is
to produce the knowledge needed to help individuals, groups, and institutions
act in an informed and enlightened manner and elevate the quality of life on
a personal level and in society as a whole.

EVALUATING POSITIVISM

The positivist orientation has contributed a great deal to the development
of the social sciences, but a careful examination of its underlying assumptions suggests that it does have some significant problems. One of its more

egregious shortcomings centers on the matter of conceptual framing in social research. The positivist ideal of gathering objective findings about the social world is rooted in an effort to transcend personal and cultural bias, where researchers are able to see the issues they are studying in a neutral or dispassionate way. This ideal is well intentioned, and there is certainly a great deal of merit in the attempt to learn more about social phenomena; however, this position does not adequately address the point that social research always takes place in relation to a starting perspective and initial set of assumptions about the issues involved and about the social world generally. The inescapable fact of the matter is that every social scientific investigation begins with a preliminary arrangement of categories that provide it with its basic structure. Even the most complex social analyses rely on a system of classification and conceptual configuration, although the researchers involved may not be aware of these. There are times when scholars can so thoroughly internalize the theoretical framework they are employing in their research that they take it for granted and lose sight of its socially constructed nature. Karl Mannheim observed this phenomenon and commented on it many years ago:

> No one denies the possibility of empirical research nor does anyone maintain that facts do not exist. (Nothing seems more incorrect to us than an illusionist theory of knowledge.) We, too, appeal to "facts" for our proof, but the question of the nature of facts is in itself a considerable problem. They exist for the mind always in an intellectual and social context. That they can be understood and formulated implies already the existence of a conceptual apparatus. And if this conceptual apparatus is the same for all the members of a group, the presuppositions (i.e. the possible social and intellectual values), which underlie the individual concepts, never become perceptible.[10]

The "conceptual apparatus" researchers rely on in their work provides the basis for their understanding of the issues involved and may become so integrated into their thinking that they lose sight of the ways they are using it in their study and in making sense of the social world. This framework is often a reflection of the commonly accepted ideas circulating in their field and in their larger social milieu, and to the extent that social scientists are aware of it, they are inclined to see it as given. The significance of this phenomenon in terms of social scientific knowledge is that it can play a powerful role in shaping the analyses and conclusions scholars develop in their investigations. This basic point runs headlong into the positivist assertion that properly gathered social scientific data directly represent the objective truth. The facts drawn from such data may be indisputable from a particular starting perspective, but when the socially constructed nature of this perspective is revealed, the potential fallibility of its associated analyses and conclusions becomes apparent as well.

The issue of the need for a starting framework brings our discussion to the matter of values in social research. A key tenet of the positivist orientation is that researchers have an obligation to approach their subject matter in a value-neutral way so they can develop the most accurate and unbiased assessment possible. Those operating from within this orientation are therefore expected to refrain from making value judgments about their topic and instead adopt the attitude of a detached observer. One of the central problems of this expectation is that it fails to acknowledge the inherent presence of values in all forms of social scientific inquiry. A few simple questions can reveal the value-laden nature of any research project by drawing attention to the unstated assumptions of the researchers themselves. For instance, one might ask researchers the following questions: Why did you choose to study this particular topic and not another? Why do you consider this topic to be important? Why have you decided to frame the issues involved in this way versus other possible ways? Why are you asking this set of research questions and not others? Researchers may try to respond to these questions in a neutral fashion and go some distance without revealing an overt connection to values, but this kind of discussion inevitably leads to the realization that some degree of value judgment is needed on the part of researchers in order to set up the project at the outset and carry it forward to a conclusion. The very act of putting together and engaging in an investigation demands that researchers decide what they will be studying and how to study it. These decisions cannot be made in a matter-of-fact or universally dispassionate way, but only on the basis of norms and values, even when creating what seems on the surface to be a completely impartial inquiry.

We can take this argument a step further to address the concerns of those who are particularly reluctant to acknowledge the presence of values in social research by adding some pressing questions to our list. For instance, we might ask: Why is it preferable to study the social world in a value-free way? Why should one work toward objectivity in social research? To the supporters of positivism, these questions need not be asked since it is understood that taking such an approach will yield more accurate information and help provide clarity regarding the issues being studied. However, this response does not answer the questions. Why is this a goal? Why should one be concerned about working toward the future enlightenment of human civilization? One can attempt to dismiss these questions on the grounds that the answers are obvious, but they are only obvious from a normative perspective that has guided social research from its inception. The positivist position is grounded in a very clear set of assumptions about what is important and situates the foundation of social science squarely in the realm of values. Social scientists continue to espouse this way of thinking and rely on it as a guide in form-ing their own research projects as well as in their analyses and criticisms of others. In this sense, even that which appears on the surface to be a detached form of social research is inherently value-laden.

Scholars operating in a positivist manner have tried to circumvent the influ-ence of values in their work in a number of ways. One attempt to do so can be seen in the development of grounded theory. The idea behind this approach is that researchers begin their investigations with a loosely defined conceptual framework and then engage in an inquiry that provides the opportunity to revise this framework as new evidence emerges. The logic of this technique is that the evidence itself produces patterns that become increasingly clear and that it is the investigator's task to observe and identify these patterns and bring them forward in the study. This allows scholars to explore issues from a less rigid framework, and it provides a useful way to reduce the influence of a priori assumptions that may be guiding the investigation.

One issue with this approach is that it does not enable researchers to side-step the use of a conceptual framework altogether. When employing this technique, researchers continue to operate on the basis of a particular mode of understanding. The fact that they are being flexible and willing to consider alternative ways to construct the topic does not eliminate the presence of a conceptual framework entirely. It merely shifts the modus operandi from using a preset perspective to one that is formed in relation to the evidence as understood by the researchers themselves. In other words, the use of grounded theory involves moving away from the practice of unconsciously relying on unstated suppositions in social research, but it continues to require investigators to eventually come up with a system of classification in order to make sense of the data they are gathering, and this cannot be done without some form of normative judgment. Thus, even when relying on grounded theory, researchers are unavoidably involved in an interpretive process requiring the use of value-laden assessments. This endeavor is quite different from the activity of simply uncovering neutral or unbiased truths about what is happening in this setting.[11]

There are some authors who have argued that it is possible to use grounded theory with an awareness of the socially constructed nature of knowledge and engage in social research in this light. This version of grounded theory provides a way for researchers to broaden their horizons by bringing the issue of a starting framework to the fore and by allowing some flexibility in this regard. Yet, even when one employs the social constructionist mode of grounded theory, there are many possible perspectives that can be used to interpret the findings. When researchers form theories to describe and explain social phenomena, they do so in relation to a particular worldview. They may perceive such constructions as direct representations of the data in their study, but in so doing, they are missing the point that these representations also contain embedded conceptual premises that provide the foundation for the way the study was put together and the culturally specific manner they have chosen to interpret that which they have observed.[12]

In addition, the language researchers rely on to make sense of their topic consists of preconceived shared meanings, and these play a principal role in shaping their conceptions of the issues involved. Even those who are aware of the constructed nature of social research have little choice but to rest their assessments on these shared meanings in comprehending the phenomena they are studying and in communicating their findings to others. Investigators may choose to construct entirely new words with qualitatively new meanings as a part of their work—and this practice can possibly serve to enhance their understandings of the issues at hand and sidestep the limitations of everyday language—but following this course of action can also lead to difficulties when attempting to communicate these analyses to others who are unfamiliar with these newer terms.[13]

In spite of these issues, the social constructionist mode of grounded theory is a step in the right direction in that it highlights the normative dimensions of social research and represents a concerted effort to move beyond the limitations of positivism. This approach to grounded theory has been one way for researchers to take the initial step toward acknowledging the conceptual foundations of social inquiry and consider alternative perspectives regarding the situations they are studying. This in itself is an important contribution to the development of a balanced epistemological orientation for social research.

Another way social scientists have attempted to circumvent the problem of a starting perspective is to standardize the methods of research in their work. The logic of this practice is centered on the idea that employing the proper set of methodologies can reduce the individual variation that can occur from one study to the next. From this point of view, doing so also serves to eliminate less rigorous methods that have shown to be problematic in the past and give a greater degree of legitimacy to those that have demonstrated their worth over time.

Taking this approach can lessen the disparity that would otherwise emerge between parallel studies on the same topic and help prevent researchers from creating poorly formed investigations. However, drawing on standardized methods of research does not enable social scientists to avoid the issue of a starting perspective altogether. It merely helps them produce studies that are relatively uniform in terms of the logic and modes of classification they subscribe to each step of the way.

In contemporary social science, for example, researchers are accustomed to using variable analysis in their work. The task of a researcher adopting this method is to identify the variables involved in a given context and examine the connections between them, taking note of the ways they shift in relation to one another. This can provide an abundance of information and yield a wide range of insightful research findings, but it can only do so within the theoretical framework used to define the variables in the first place. Herbert Blumer raised this issue long ago in an essay entitled "Sociological Analysis and the Variable," in which he pointed out that the act of identifying a variable is one that cannot be carried out in a value-neutral manner.[14] In this essay, Blumer stated that this task necessarily involves deciding how to partition various dimensions of the social world and form a definition for each of these dimensions in a way that is seen as acceptable to one's colleagues and others evaluating the validity of the study. This is a normative endeavor and can only be undertaken in conjunction with specific conceptions linked to a particular perspective. Scholars using this method typically consider a variable to be legitimate when it makes sense to them and possesses some degree of reliability within a given discipline. This may lead them to take standard definitions as given and miss the culturally specific nature of their inquiry and of the analyses and conclusions they draw. As researchers tabulate the data and look for patterns and correlations, the interpretive dimensions of their investigations fade into the background and take a less prominent role. These initial ambiguities may come out as the work is reviewed by others, but only if those doing the reviewing have the insight and knowledge of the practices involved to recognize the constructed nature of the variables used in the first place. This is unlikely to occur in a field if the assumptions and beliefs about the topic being studied are consistent with those of the researchers and reviewers alike.[15]

In addition, people outside academia typically do not have the understanding of research methods needed to adequately scrutinize this process and are therefore prone to interpret such findings as absolute, particularly when the initial framework resonates with ideas that are commonly accepted in their own culture. Research carried out in this manner can indeed reveal new information about the social world, but it does so in relation to certain cultural norms and values—as do all investigations in the social sciences.

Another problem with variable analysis is that while it is grounded in an effort to facilitate new knowledge on a particular topic, it can also limit the breadth of understanding that emerges from the investigations where it is used. It can lead researchers to shift their focus away from studying social phenomena that are less tangible and toward those that are more readily identifiable and measurable. Developing an initial assessment of a topic typically involves identifying aspects of it that are not empirically isolable and therefore not easily adapted to the variable analysis approach. This can lead researchers to shy away from focusing on the less concrete dimensions of a project out of a concern that bringing these in could create methodological weaknesses and jeopardize the integrity of the study in the long run. While this is a legitimate practice in that it can yield more precise and clearly defined variables, it can also narrow the focus of an investigation to the point where it offers limited insight into the topic being studied and leaves out potentially valuable information. The requirement that investigators restrict their studies to variables that can be delineated in a distinct manner has the potential to lead them to overlook key aspects of the situations they are observing, and this can interfere with the development of broader under-standings of that issue. The social world is much more complex than variable analysis and the positivist methods of research can show. The practice of social scientists seeking out very specific dimensions surrounding an area of social life can indeed reveal something about the relationship between those dimensions, but it can also project the notion that it has captured the totality of the phenomena being studied, when, in fact, it has not. This draws atten-tion away from aspects of the social milieu that are present but not addressed in the study and therefore absent in the conclusion and in the body of social scientific knowledge generally.

In light of this critique of variable analysis, it is also important to point out that this type of research is capable of uncovering valuable information about larger societal trends. This is to say that there are times when variable analysis yields knowledge of the social world that surpasses that which can be obtained via other methods. This approach can help researchers gather information about the factors involved in shaping social phenomena and yield findings that are not readily apparent to the casual observer. Studies employ-ing variable analysis can, for instance, identify disparities in health care opportunities that may exist from one group to another or demonstrate the extent to which social stratification influences the life chances of members of lower class groups in a particular context. Although this method has its short-comings, it can nevertheless provide an important way to gather and analyze information that is inaccessible using informal or experiential observation. The important point to stress in this regard is that while variable analysis has the potential to offer insight into important social phenomena, the tendency of researchers to treat normative concepts as if they were culturally neutral gives the impression that their research is purely objective, even in instances when it is not. Blumer's main argument is not that variable analysis is universally problematic as a method in the social sciences, but that it is often used in ways that do not meet the scientific criterion of what constitutes a variable. This practice gives the impression that concrete scientific work is being done and obscures the interpretive nature of the research involved.[16]

This discussion brings us to what is perhaps one of the more significant epistemological shortcomings of the positivist orientation, and that is its potential to overlook the personal dimensions of everyday life. As researchers seek to investigate the social world in an objective manner, they are prone to bypass its subjective or human character. Embracing this orientation in the pursuit of objectivity can lead investigators to ignore features of the situation they are studying that do not help them work toward this goal. When doing so, they can fail to capture aspects of that situation that are essential to understanding it more fully. This approach may enable researchers to identify phenomena that are relevant to the study, but it can also push them to construct a view of their subject matter that is foreign to lived experience.[17] Researchers may arrive at conclusions that appear to be insightful from one perspective, but lacking insight from another. When attempting to objectify human interaction, they can miss much of what they claim to have captured and pass on that limited assessment to their peers and others drawing on the results of the investigation. The irony of this practice is that while it is motivated by an interest in developing a broad understanding of the social world, it can actually foster a narrow view of it in the long run.[18]

This takes us back to the issue of the relationship between social science and politics as it relates to the positivist orientation. While many contemporary researchers reject the Comtean idea that social scientific knowledge can serve as a direct guide in the formation of public policy, the underlying logic of this belief still endures in the social sciences today. Many researchers approach their subject matter in the hopes that their findings will ultimately have some influence outside academia, whether this takes place indirectly through the gradual dissemination of their research findings or directly as in cases where results and conclusions are utilized by public policymakers, members of the judiciary, or other institutional leaders.

These hopes are certainly justified, and there is much to be said for the assertion that social scientists are well suited to offer public policy recommendations. After all, social scientists have devoted their lives to studying social phenomena and have collectively learned a great deal over the course of many generations. It seems reasonable to recommend that this knowledge be used in a practical way. The fact of the matter is that it has been used in varying stages throughout modern history and into the present. The use of social scientific knowledge in the realm of public policy is in itself not a problem, but there are some issues that arise when one considers the relationship between these two.

The first of these issues has to do with the integrity of the research and the independence of the investigators involved. When researchers approach a topic because they are innately interested in it and are genuinely open to learning about that topic, the study itself and the findings it yields have the potential to offer a substantial contribution to the development of social scientific knowledge. When their motivations for doing a study are intimately connected to an interest in working toward new knowledge, the possibility of reaching that goal becomes much more viable. However, if the original impetus to do the study is related to an interest in advancing a preset political agenda, the potential for bias grows, and the overall independence of the study can be compromised. The question then is not simply about the connections between social science and politics but the nature of these connections and their influence on the conclusions developed and actions taken in conjunction with those conclusions.

The significance of this phenomenon as it relates to the positivist orientation is that when researchers believe they are gathering factual information, they are prone to seeing themselves as impervious to such pressures and tend to characterize their findings as infallible because the work is objective. But as we have seen, the fact that all social scientific investigations rely on a perspective means that there is a very real possibility that the researchers involved may be influenced by the conditions associated with the support of the project itself. Under these circumstances, their findings can drift from the domain of scientific knowledge into that of political knowledge.[19]

The irony of this situation is that while positivist researchers generally embrace the goal of forming unbiased assessments, their belief in the infallibility of social science may actually undermine that goal by leading them to participate in projects that have subtle but influential motives attached to them, thereby interfering with the neutrality and perspicacity of their work on the whole.

Having devoted our attention to the weaknesses of positivism, it seems only fair to reflect on the dimensions of this orientation that have benefited the social sciences and the sphere of knowledge generally. Positivism is limited in many respects, but it has contributed to the development of social thought and to the directions of contemporary social science throughout modernity. One of the principal consequences of a reliance on the positivist orientation in social science is that it has pushed researchers to seek empirically grounded analyses and challenge the validity of poorly formed or unsubstantiated ideas. For all its flaws, positivism has nurtured a drive in social scientists to get to the heart of the issues they are studying and find new ways to make sense of the social world. Social scientists are notorious for their reluctance to accept truth claims at face value. They are well known for their tendency to challenge commonly held beliefs and critically evaluate taken-for-granted assumptions and cultural practices. One could argue that the positivist undertones of social science have helped researchers set a very high standard for what they consider to be truth. The demand that all assertions be supported by empirical evidence and reasoned thinking has enhanced the debates surrounding political and economic issues and pushed scholars to form new and important insight into the dynamics of contemporary social life. This knowledge has certainly been fallible at times, but it has nevertheless offered a way to challenge conventional beliefs and provide the substantive information needed to develop informed alternatives. Human history has demonstrated the potential of people around the world to accept inaccurate or blatantly false claims as truth and rely on such claims in making decisions about how to act at the personal and institutional levels. The attitude of skepticism embedded in the positivist philosophy has helped challenge this pattern and provide the conceptual tools needed to learn about social phenomena in a meaningful and enlightened manner. In spite of its epistemological flaws, positivism has raised the stakes in the quest for new understanding and contributed to the ongoing development of innovative and insightful knowledge about the social world broadly.

Positivism has thus served as an influential orientation for the social sciences throughout the modern era. It has provided a way of thinking that at times goes against the current of mainstream thought and challenges the foundations of everyday practice. Social scientists rely on it to appraise speculative assertions and demand that all statements be supported empirically and through logical reasoning. It has, in this sense, nurtured the development of a higher standard in the formation of knowledge about the contemporary social world. This epistemological orientation has put pressure on researchers to engage in their investigations in rigorous and thought-provoking ways and enabled them to cut through some of the common but unsubstantiated myths circulating in a variety of contemporary cultures, thereby enriching our collective understanding on a range of topics and social issues.

Even social scientists who do not themselves overtly identify with the principles of the positivist tradition routinely adopt the spirit of this orientation in their day-to-day habits of thought, as for example when they refuse to accept assertions at face value or when they call into question the reasoning of a particular argument. The ongoing tradition of employing positivist thinking in academia and beyond has raised the level of debate on public issues and facilitated the development of new knowledge about individual lives and the social world generally.

Nevertheless, when we apply that same spirit of critique to the positivist habits of thought and practice in the social sciences, we can see that there are some very salient value-laden assumptions associated with this orientation, and these shape the nature of social scientific knowledge as well. If social scientists are willing to consider the possibility that their ways of understanding the social world are culturally normative and grounded in a particular set of values, they are in a better position to develop strategies to improve these approaches and elevate the quality of their work overall.

Recognizing the perspectival nature of social science does not lead us to the simplistic belief that social research is incapable of revealing insightful conclusions about the social world. On the contrary, when social research is conducted in an open-minded and theoretically informed manner, it can yield findings that are of a higher caliber than those formed on the basis of speculation or limited experience. There will always be some degree of value judgment in social scientific analysis, but this does not mean that researchers cannot develop new insight when relying on this in their work.

The positivist orientation has helped strengthen our knowledge of the social world, but its contributions must also be seen in the context of its shortcomings and in relation to the interpretive nature of social science. By acknowledging the central weaknesses of positivism, we are not diminishing the value of social scientific knowledge generally, but moving toward the development of a more subtle epistemological orientation for social research that recognizes its human dimensions and supports the ongoing effort to more fully understand the world around us.

NOTES

1. For further insight into Comte's ideas, please see: Auguste Comte, *System of Positive Polity* (London: Longmans, Green, and Co., 1875). This collection was condensed and translated by Harriet Martineau with the title *The Positive Philosophy of Auguste Comte* (London: George Bell & Sons, 1896).

2. Comte, *The Positive Philosophy*, 1–12.

3. Comte, *The Positive Philosophy*, 29.

4. This quote is from Auguste Comte, *Plan of Scientific Operations Necessary for Reorganizing Society*, reprinted in Phillip Rieff, ed., *On Intellectuals: Theoretical Studies, Case Studies* (Garden City, NY: Anchor Books, 1970), 252–53.

5. Comte, *The Positive Philosophy*, 10–59.

6. Comte quoted in Rieff, *On Intellectuals*, 277.

7. Comte quoted in Rieff, *On Intellectuals*, 277.

8. Comte, *The Positive Philosophy*, 1–29.

9. There have been many variations of positivist thought since the time of Comte's writing, some echoing his ideas and others revising this line of thinking. Examples include those writing in the early twentieth century as part of the Vienna Circle. Members of this group sought to develop an alternative to positivism that emphasized the use of logic along with empirical investigation, calling it Logical Positivism. Social thinkers in this camp include Ernst Mach, Moritz Schlick, Philipp Frank, Rudolf Carnap, and many others. For a thorough overview of the ideas of authors in the Vienna Circle, please see: Friedrich Stadler, *The Vienna Circle: Studies in the Origins, Development, and Influence of Logical Empiricism* (New York, NY: Springer, 2015). Also: Otto Neurath, J. Hahn, and R. Carnap, "The Scientific Conception of the World: The Vienna Circle," in *Empiricism and Sociology*, ed. M. Neurath and R. S. Cohen (Dordrecht: Reidel, 1973), 299–318. Another author writing in the positivist tradition is Jonathan Turner. For a thorough understanding

of Turner's position on this topic, please see: Jonathan H. Turner, "In Defense of Positivism," *Sociological Theory* 3, no. 2 (Autumn, 1985): 24–30.

10. Karl Mannheim, *Ideology and Utopia, An Introduction to the Sociology of Knowledge* (New York, NY: Harcourt, Brace & World, 1968), 102.

11. For more on this initial form of grounded theory, please see: Barney Glaser and Anselm Strauss, *The Discovery of Grounded Theory: Strategies for Qualitative Research* (Chicago, IL: Aldine, 1967).

12. For more on the constructionist form of grounded theory, please see: Kathy Charmaz, *Constructing Grounded Theory* (New York, NY: Sage, 2014).

13. The connections between language and the framing of social issues will be discussed further in subsequent chapters of this book. Specifically, chapter 2 begins with a discussion of the ideas of Franz Boas and his position regarding the ties between language and social research. Chapter 3 examines the work of hermeneutical scholars and their claims about the subtle ways language provides the foundation for knowledge of the social world. Also, a section in chapter 4 outlines the analyses of Husserl and Schütz and their ideas about language as the basis for shared meanings and mutual understanding.

14. Please see: Herbert Blumer, "Sociological Analysis and the Variable," *American Sociological Review* 21 (1956): 683–90.

15. Blumer, "Sociological Analysis," 683–90.

16. Blumer, "Sociological Analysis," 683–90.

17. For more on standpoint theory, please see: Dorothy Smith, "Methods of Writing Patriarchy," in *Feminism and Sociological Theory*, ed. Ruth Wallace (Newbury Park, CA: Sage, 1989), 34–64.

18. Smith, "Methods of Writing Patriarchy," 34–64.

19. One can characterize this process as the politicization of knowledge and science. A thorough examination of this issue can be found in the work of Max Weber and Karl Mannheim. Please see two essays by Max Weber: "Science as a Vocation," and "Politics as a Vocation," in *From Max Weber: Essays in Sociology*, trans. Hans Gerth and C. Wright Mills (New York, NY: Oxford University Press, 1958; orig. pub. 1919), 77–156. Mannheim addresses this issue in *Ideology and Utopia*, 125–69. Please also see: Charles F. Gattone, *The Social Scientist as Public Intellectual: Critical Reflections in a Changing World* (New York, NY: Rowman & Littlefield, 2006).

Chapter 2

Relativism

Truth in the Eye of the Beholder

Now that we have taken a look at the positivist orientation, let us move on to a discussion of relativism to identify some of its characteristics and consider its strengths and weaknesses as they relate to the social sciences. Perhaps the best way to begin this assessment is to state at the outset that there is not one set of principles associated with relativism. This is an umbrella term encompassing a wide range of perspectives and an eclectic mix of ideas. It is therefore necessary to acknowledge this variation and come face to face with the inherent problems involved in attempting to discuss this term generally. This diversity poses a challenge to anyone trying to describe and evaluate relativism, but it does not preclude the possibility of any discussion at all. There are some common characteristics embedded in this orientation, and in this chapter, I focus on these commonalities to identify and appraise this rather loosely defined set of concepts and assertions.

CULTURAL RELATIVISM

Before delving into a general characterization of relativism, however, we must first draw a distinction between that which is typically characterized as "cultural relativism" and the broader notion of "philosophical relativism" since these two are somewhat different in terms of their emphases and areas of focus.

Cultural relativism is an orientation that has served as the basis for a variety of social scientific work—particularly anthropological research—since the early part of the twentieth century. One of its central premises is that researchers studying unfamiliar social groups may be inclined to unwittingly draw on the norms, values, beliefs, and traditions of their home culture in an effort to make sense of their observations. This can lead them to form narrow or poorly constructed analyses and fail to understand people on their own terms. Within the framework of cultural relativism, the goal of social research is to learn more about different ways of life as seen through the eyes of the people embedded in a particular culture rather than from the perspectives of the researchers themselves.[1]

Franz Boas helped establish this orientation in anthropological research, arguing that seeking to understand people from their own point of view was consistent with the goals of social science in that it entailed moving beyond the limitations of one's own cultural boundaries. He saw language as a major component of culture, arguing that language is reflective of the ways people make sense of their experiences and form meaningful conceptions of the world around them. Boas argued that language is of particular importance to social science in that it frames the assumptions that serve as the starting point for understanding people in their own milieu.[2]

Boas was critical of the tendency of some researchers to engage in varying levels of ethnocentrism—where the inclination is to perceive one's own culture as inherently superior to others—and he pointed to instances where investigators assumed they were operating in a neutral manner when, in fact, they were employing subtle forms of bias. He railed against the idea of characterizing certain cultures as primitive and others as advanced, seeing this as a normative conceptualization that is blind to its value-laden underpinnings. He was similarly critical of the scientific racism of his day, where researchers constructed biological explanations for the differences in thought and behavior they observed in the groups they studied, citing physical characteristics and racial background as determining traits such as intelligence or disposition.[3]

Boas proposed an alternative to these practices in his suggestion that researchers view instances of cultural variation between groups as related to the situational factors and social influences involved. To support this idea, he pointed to the variation that can exist from one culture to the next, even among people who are considered to be of the same ethnic or racial constitution. He argued that cultural norms can be a powerful force in shaping the inclinations of people living in a particular community or geographic region. Social factors are, in this way of thinking, much more significant than the imagined biological influence of race or ethnicity in shaping people's worldviews, traditions, and actions.[4]

Boas also rejected the notion that the principal goal of social science is to develop universal laws about the social world. He proposed, instead, that researchers focus on the particular social characteristics of the groups they are studying and work toward the development of context-specific analyses and conclusions. He held the position that the faith of researchers in their ability to discover universal truths reflected an implicit view of people as inanimate objects, behaving in consistently uniform ways and unlikely to deviate from established patterns or expectations. Boas observed the extraordinarily divergent nature of culture, arguing that the effort to generalize from one context to the next presumes a level of uniformity across cultural boundaries that simply does not exist.[5]

Proponents of cultural relativism claim that it has been valuable as a guide in the social sciences generally. Its strength, in this sense, can be found in the notion that when researchers consciously refrain from employing their own normative assumptions, they are better able to understand the groups they are investigating. In cases where researchers fail to recognize the extent to which their own cultural leanings are influencing their analyses, they are inclined to form conclusions that are not only misguided but also lacking in the ability to move beyond the barriers that separate one group from the next.

In contrast to these favorable assessments, cultural relativism has also received its share of critique. One common complaint is that while the goal of seeking to understand people from an insider's perspective is desirable, the potential of investigators to transcend their own cultural bias is limited. Researchers may convince themselves that they are bridging cultural differences when, in fact, they are continuing to rely on their own conceptual frames in their analyses and misunderstanding the ideas, values, and beliefs of the people they are studying.[6]

From this point of view, any attempt to understand the experiences of others requires a double leap of faith. The first involves the belief that one is capable of grasping the inner sentiment of others as reflected in their language, behavior, or various forms of communication. The second is the assumption that the researcher's mindset can connect with that of the individual or group being studied. The challenges inherent in navigating these obstacles lessen the potential for genuine understanding across cultural boundaries.[7]

In addition, critics of cultural relativism argue that employing this approach in the examination of non-Western cultures can lead researchers to essentialize the people in the study by assuming a level of uniformity in the group that does not exist. Although cultural relativists may be open to considering differences from one culture to the next, they are prone to glossing over variation within a specific group, developing analyses that are oversimplified and conveying a distorted image of the people involved.[8]

In response to these criticisms, advocates of cultural relativism state that while there are certainly some difficulties in seeking to understand cultures outside one's own, it is not impossible to work in this direction. They point out that social research embracing the idea of cultural relativism does not always overlook the variation within specific groups and that countless ethnographic studies have brought about an abundance of insight into ways of life that were either completely unknown or poorly understood.[9]

When considering the sum of these competing arguments, one cannot deny that cultural relativism has served as an effective and essential guide for the social sciences. Its principal strength lies in its attention to the inherent value in seeking to learn about people from an insider's point of view and in avoiding the practice of imposing one's own normative judgments on the individuals and groups being studied.

PHILOSOPHICAL RELATIVISM

This brings the focus of our discussion to philosophical relativism and its many diverse and, at times, competing ideas. At a fundamental level, we can describe philosophical relativism as a skepticism toward truth claims and the possibility of being able to attain any degree of objectivity, whether this is universal or context specific. Truth seen in this light is best understood as a matter of personal viewpoint or individual belief.

In order to work toward a deeper understanding of this rather elusive and multifaceted set of concepts, we can look at the writings of scholars who have contributed to its formation in one way or another. Those discussed in this chapter should not be read as "pure" relativists, since the ideas of most social thinkers are not uniformly deserving of this title. Even those whose writings seem to embody the essence of relativism can weave in and out of it at times, precluding the possibility of placing them in a distinct category called "relativist." Nevertheless, there are some whose conceptualizations are closer to relativism than others, and we will discuss their work with a particular focus on aspects of their thought that venture in this direction. Hopefully, this will give us a better understanding of relativism and its ties to epistemology in the social sciences.

FRIEDRICH NIETZSCHE

One author whose writings exhibit elements of this orientation is the German philosopher Friedrich Nietzsche. Nietzsche was one of the more complex and enigmatic intellectuals of the Western world. His tendency to hover around a theme in a circuitous fashion and present ideas using innuendo and narrative leaves the reader with the challenge of having to sort through and find meaning in a mix of what appear to be conflicting points and counterpoints. Rather than simply identifying an issue and forming a position on that issue, Nietzsche often relied on allusion and suggestion as a way to convey his arguments implicitly. We can read this practice not as an indication of a lack of perspective, but as a sign of a subtle thinker who is not easily observed, analyzed, or labeled. Taking this approach in our venture into Nietzsche's world enables us to get a bit closer to understanding his epistemological position and its connections to relativism in the social sciences.

One of the narratives Nietzsche conveyed in his writings refers to ancient civilizations and the desire of warrior aristocracies to legitimate their authority in their own eyes and from the point of view of their subjects. Nietzsche maintained that, in these settings, having wealth, property, and dominion over others came to be seen as an indication of an inherent superiority, while being poor, disenfranchised, or subjugated meant one was weak and inferior. The destitute and powerless were, in this light, pitiful and looked down upon, while those with power were seen as strong, successful, and deserving of praise. Nietzsche called this perspective the "master morality," characterizing it as one that prevailed throughout much of ancient history, giving leaders an element of bravado in their accomplishments, and justifying their advantageous position over others.[10]

Those who found themselves at the mercy of the ruling classes in this context reacted to their plight in a variety of ways. Some embraced the master morality, seeing their leaders' power as a sign of greatness and taking significant pride in being among their subjects. Others facing these conditions forged an analysis that resonated with their experience of being oppressed— one that viewed their own plight as enduring harsh treatment under the weight of excessive domination.[11] From the latter perspective, being powerless was a fate unjustly thrust upon them, forcing them into a life that was cruel and unwarranted. Those in this position did not seek to dominate others or cause harm to anyone, but instead sought a more peaceful and fair existence. Yet, in spite of their efforts to attain this goal, they were forced to endure mistreatment and abuse from their superiors. For their suffering, they were seen as deserving of recognition and as being among the righteous and the good. Nietzsche called this the "slave morality" and suggested it countered the "master morality" by turning it on its head, framing those who were "bad" as now "good" and those who had been labeled "good" as now "evil."[12]

He further argued that the Judeo-Christian belief system endorsed the slave morality and strengthened it over time. As this belief system expanded, it helped the slave morality flourish to the point where it eventually came to dominate the values of Western culture. Nietzsche maintained that this perspective depicted suffering as an unjust and unnecessary part of life that needed to be explained in some way. The result was to view suffering as sacrifice, where those who suffered were seen as martyrs and as giving up their own potential well-being for the sake of some higher good. People who engaged in sacrifice were, from this vantage point, worthy of admiration and revered as iconic figures who had earned a position of true greatness.[13]

In Nietzsche's view, depicting suffering in this manner helped uplift it by condoning it and making it virtuous, thereby fostering its perpetuation and expansion. The Judeo-Christian belief system helped establish the slave morality as a guiding ethos for a righteous way of life throughout the West and in other parts of the world as well. It bolstered the legitimacy of this perspective and gave credence to the idea that suffering itself was a pathway to human fulfillment.[14]

Nietzsche further argued that the slave morality, as a component of the Judeo-Christian tradition, contributed to the idea that there is a degree of holiness in seeking to live an ascetic life—one that shuns material possessions or indulgence in physical pleasures of any kind. Asceticism is a means through which to work toward piety and achieve an advanced level of spirituality. In Nietzsche's view, "the ascetic ideal" had become an integral component of the slave morality and informed the Judeo-Christian values of simplicity, sanctity, and salvation.[15]

Nietzsche observed and analyzed the practices of secular philosophers and scientists who claimed to be the "opponents of the ascetic ideal."[16] He suggested that they saw themselves as purveyors of Enlightenment thought and as having transcended the older, mythological ways of viewing the world. He challenged this assertion, proposing that, in their strict demand for scholarly purity, secular philosophers and scientists were eager to fulfill the ascetic ideal through their own unyielding dedication to the pursuit of truth. From his point of view, "this ideal is precisely their ideal too."[17] The idea of operating at the level of objectivity is, in Nietzsche's analysis, motivated by a quest for clarity and a desire to stand above the mundane and routine dimensions of everyday life. Being able to achieve a detached demeanor is seen as transcending the limits of routine experience and as possessing an elevated awareness relative to those who are caught up in the prevailing habits of thought and action typical of a particular cultural group.[18]

Nietzsche did not suggest that he had somehow managed to escape the ascetic ideal, but claimed that he himself was inclined toward an ascetic life as well.[19] He proposed that while he could not completely ignore his own past, in choosing to confront that past, he was able to become more aware of what motivated and underscored his instincts. Acknowledging his own training in the ascetic ideal, Nietzsche claimed to have become better able to recognize it in his own thought and take this into consideration when making judgments and life decisions. He wrote that being a philosopher requires one to employ some degree of self-discipline and internal critique, where the ability to attain "self-mastery" is strengthened. In this somewhat roundabout manner, Nietzsche managed to avoid adopting a simplistic good-versus-evil stance in relation to the ascetic ideal. Instead, he sought to reveal its presence to the reader and bring forth its complexities and contradictions, while at the same time acknowledging his own involvement in it.[20]

Nietzsche also maintained that the Judeo-Christian faith in the existence of a Supreme Being provided the foundation for a secular belief in absolute truth. In this tradition, God is all-powerful and all-knowing and therefore has an unbridled comprehension of all reality. It would be blasphemous from this point of view to assume that God was capable of anything less. Believing in a single, all-powerful God possessing a complete grasp of all knowledge means that there is such a thing as absolute objectivity. From this perspective, the existence of a transcendent world is taken to be a priori, and the concept of multiple realities existing simultaneously becomes inherently false. Relying on this epistemological starting point leads to the conclusion that the only tenable position is one that uncritically accepts the existence of a higher truth. In Nietzsche's eyes, the Judeo-Christian belief system thus helped strengthen the notion that there is only one real truth and that this truth exists in a neutral space, independent of whether human beings understand it or not.[21]

Nietzsche suggested that this perspective came to supersede all others in Western thought and informed the logic of scientific discovery. The quest for truth, as manifested in the domain of science, gradually came to serve as a substitute for theism. He maintained that the notion of transcending the mundane world is tied to a faith in the ability of science to go beyond the limitations of everyday understanding and to bring us closer to enlightenment and an awareness of the one and only transcendent reality.[22]

Part of what has been retained from this legacy is a set of values that are so ingrained in the scientific mind that they are typically unnoticed. The merits involved in searching for truth are rarely questioned. Instead, the virtue of this quest is taken to be outside the realm of value judgment and as an indisputable component of scientific inquiry.[23]

Nietzsche drew a connection between the "will to truth" and the desire to preserve a specific type of existence. Although presented as a neutral search for what is real, the will to truth is based on a set of values or beliefs such as "the definite is preferable to the indefinite." He argued, for example, that to scholars such as Socrates, error is the "evil par excellence," and the search for truth is the noblest of all virtues. In response to this assertion, Nietzsche proclaimed that error is an integral part of life and that veils are crucial to understanding.[24]

In his account of the presumed existence of absolute truth, Nietzsche also criticized the perspective of thinkers who abided by the mantra "all is to be doubted," for this was, to him, related to the belief that one can overcome illusion. He scoffed at atheists and their dogmatic belief in the "truth" that there is no God.

Unqualified honest atheism (and its air only do we breathe, we, the most intellectual men of this age) is not opposed to that ideal, to the extent that it appears
to be; it is rather one of the final phases of its evolution, one of its syllogisms and
pieces of inherent logic—it is the awe-inspiring catastrophe of a two-thousand-
year training in truth, which finally forbids itself *the lie of the belief in God.*[25]

The assertion of secular philosophers that belief in God is necessarily false
is grounded in an implicit faith in the possibility of absolute truth and falsity.
The notion of universal truth—itself tied to a Judeo-Christian perspective—
reveals its normative roots in atheism's steadfast denial of God's existence.[26]

Nietzsche suggested that traditional Enlightenment philosophers and their
followers in the arena of science failed to understand that rather than fostering an environment where human qualities had the opportunity to grow and
flourish, their efforts contributed to the formation of a highly rationalized
and mechanistic world—one where efficiency and material progress took
center stage. He argued that this way of thinking demonstrated a basic naivete
regarding the nature of life itself. It failed to recognize that life is much more
than this, that the human dimensions of life involve not only reason and rationality, but also emotion and absurdity, aesthetics, and irrationality, and that it
is often unpredictable, ironic, and, at times, tragic. He maintained that having
faith in an increasingly reasoned and rationalized world reflected a limited
vision of human existence and ignored or repressed aspects of it that did not
fit neatly into this view.[27]

Nietzsche turned to Greek mythology to conjure an alternative to this perspective, referring to the gods Apollo and Dionysus to support his position.
He saw Apollo as one who represented the journey into music, poetry, and
art, and as bringing forth a measure of understanding that facilitated healing,
wisdom, and knowledge.

Apollo, the god of all plastic energies, is at the same time the soothsaying god.
He, who . . . is the "shining one," the deity of light, is also ruler over the beautiful illusion of the inner world of fantasy.[28]

Apollo governed the worlds of myth and imagination, offering a means of
understanding that served as a pathway to a more stable and reasonable
existence. This god stood for reason, logic, and rationality, and fostered the
wisdom needed to maintain order and purity—ideals enlightenment thinkers
hoped to instill in the new modern order.[29]

On the other side of the spectrum stood Dionysus. Nietzsche characterized
Dionysus as horrifying, beautiful, ugly, full of joy—an abyss. The Dionysian
is pain and contradiction. It is without form or distinction. It is that which precedes all cognition, calculation, and reason. It is life in all its chaos, glory, and

mystery, and at the same time, it is amorphous and void of meaning. Rather than shun the Dionysian, Nietzsche sought to acknowledge and accept it in all its horror and beauty as a way to affirm life. The way to reach the Dionysian is not with the crude and stiff hand of a single-minded and culturally narrow moral code, but through its dreamlike dance with the Apollonian. This is the basis of tragic wisdom from Nietzsche's standpoint. He sought to draw attention to the need to be open to life's chaotic and often puzzling features rather than hide from them or try to diminish them. Welcoming the interplay between the Apollonian and the Dionysian is, from his point of view, the way to do this.[30]

> I was the first to see the real opposition: the degenerating instinct that turns against life with subterranean vengefulness (Christianity, the philosophy of Schopenhauer, in a certain sense already the philosophy of Plato, and all of idealism as typical forms) versus a formula for the highest affirmation, born of fullness, of overfullness, a Yes-saying without reservation, even to suffering, even to guilt, even to everything that is questionable and strange in existence.[31]

Nietzsche did not seek to tear down all epistemological foundations, but to highlight the normative nature of traditional Enlightenment thinking and propose an alternative in the interplay of the Dionysian and Apollonian as a more subtle and dynamic way to understand the beauty, joy, and tragedy of everyday life.[32]

A key component of Nietzsche's analysis in this regard is his emphasis on the struggle between competing perspectives as an indication of a broader social phenomenon. In his view, competition in the world of ideas can be understood as an indirect and often hidden manifestation of "the will to power." Asserting the validity of a particular viewpoint or way of life is an imposition of a desire to influence others and bring them around to one's preferred modes of thought and action. Nietzsche sought to expose the presence of conflict in struggles between different interpretations—not to give merit to conflict generally, but to acknowledge what the modern worldview tends to ignore or deny. He sought to reveal the extent to which this perspective involves the imposition of will and the longing to control others. Although the logic of science emphasizes the value in maintaining a dispassionate stance, when one looks at it more carefully, the presence of a desire to influence others becomes evident. Nietzsche did not seek to condone or condemn this phenomenon, but to simply draw attention to it and show how the practice of scientific research is never a completely neutral endeavor.[33]

Rather than accepting the idea that there can only be one correct way to view any social situation, Nietzsche leaned toward the idea of multiple realities, where a variety of perspectives can exist simultaneously. We see in his writings that he had an affinity for multidimensional understandings of the world. He did not attempt to assert the notion that everything could be explained in a comprehensive, universal manner, but that knowledge is connected to the limitations and opportunities inherent in one viewpoint or another.

Nietzsche used the word "horizon" when discussing this issue, characterizing it as a way of seeing the world that gives shape to understanding.[34] He did not claim to be personally void of a horizon in his own analysis, but consciously adopted one that was recognizable as his own. Rather than take the untenable position that taking positions is impossible, he openly acknowledged that his positions were, in fact, positions—nothing more and nothing less. In his words, "It is now known from the outset how very much these are after all only—my truths."[35] Nietzsche did not claim that his ways of seeing the world were the only ways, but rather that they were like beads of water in an endless sea, floating among an infinite array of others, intermingling, and changing shape over time.

Nietzsche characterized the concept of objectivity "not as 'contemplation without interest' (which is a nonsensical absurdity), but as the ability to control one's Pro and Con and to dispose of them, so that one knows how to employ a variety of perspectives and affective interpretations in the service of knowledge."[36] From Nietzsche's vantage point, life teaches us things that an affinity for observation, reason, and calculation cannot. He argued that one's ability to understand the world involves more than cognition. "Ultimately, nobody can get more out of things, including books than he already knows. For what one lacks access to from experience one will have no ear."[37]

Nietzsche maintained that while the quest for absolute truth seeks an ever-increasing certainty, its limitations eventually become visible. He suggested that an awareness of these limitations can lead to a deeper sense of the ethereal nature of human existence. Quieting the calls within us that sanctify the search for exactness and letting go of the need to find concrete, all-encompassing solutions to problems can lead to the possibility of developing new insight into the contradictions and absurdities of everyday life. When life is understood as artistic expression and as a balance between the rational and irrational, its human side can be more apparent and our understanding of it enhanced.

MICHEL FOUCAULT

The social philosopher Michel Foucault picked up on many of Nietzsche's ideas and brought them into the context of the societal transformations taking place in the twentieth century. Foucault focused on the unique forms of institutional power that had emerged during this time, and he observed a link between this power arrangement and the values, morality, and cultural frames that prevailed in this setting. He argued that there is a connection between the material conditions in a given society and the kinds of ideas that become dominant within the confines of these conditions, and he studied the ways these intersections provided the foundation for social norms, consciousness, and the lives of individuals on a personal level.[38]

Foucault's positions are grounded in a view of history that rejects the idea of the inevitable advance of civilization. He saw large-scale societal transformations as instances of rupture and reorganization, where qualitatively new power dynamics and ways of living emerge in each case. From this perspective, no society is inherently superior or inferior to any other, but each is unique, with its own politics, culture, and economy. He suggested that drawing a distinction between what is thought of as "primitive" or "advanced" requires one to establish the criteria involved in making this determination and that this can only be carried out in a culturally normative fashion. In Foucault's analysis, what is seen as progress from one point of view may be understood as decline or regression from another. The process of evaluating various ways of life is fundamentally subjective and cannot be done in a neutral or dispassionate manner.[39]

Foucault maintained that every system of organization has an associated "episteme" that serves to provide an orienting framework for people living in that place and time.[40] He did not see the prevailing political-economic-cultural system as an independent entity causing the rise of this episteme, but as part of an interconnected power/consciousness web. The bonds between power and consciousness in any given social order are so intertwined that they do not exist independently of one another, but are as one. Foucault stated that "each society has its own régime of truth, its 'general politics' of truth" where what is deemed to be true is intimately connected to the institutions, culture, and interpersonal dynamics of that society.[41]

> The important thing here, I believe, is that truth isn't outside power, or lacking in power: contrary to a myth whose history and functions would repay further study, truth isn't the reward of free spirits, the child of protracted solitude, nor the privilege of those who have succeeded in liberating themselves. Truth is a thing of this world: it is produced only by virtue of multiple forms of constraint.[42]

Foucault examined the connections between truth and power sociologically by looking at the different ways this relationship manifested itself from one setting to the next. He argued that people living within a particular society come to embrace the dominant worldview of that society so fully that they typically fail to see its influence in their lives. Not realizing that they are bound by their own perspectives and practices, most view these as given and act in ways that lead them to unwittingly become a part of the system in place, even when this system oppresses them. Internalizing the prevailing worldview eases them into a naively passive state, where they are inclined to accept the legitimacy of institutional authority. These "docile bodies" become cogs in the wheels of the machine, helping to strengthen it as it grows and expands its influence in their lives.[43]

The conventions of thought and action associated with each epoch in human history come to prevail over not only those who languish in the lower echelons of society but members of the ruling elite as well. Although powerful groups may be inclined to promote a particular worldview because it resonates with their collective interests and goals, over time, the system subtly guides them toward a more thorough adherence to its illusions and demands. The institutional arrangement of every political-economic-cultural system offers new opportunities but also imposes specific constraints on those living in it, including members of the upper classes. They are ironically among its most ardent supporters, believing the myths they have helped create and failing to see that the machine they have constructed has also taken over their own lives, binding them in ways they do not understand.[44]

Foucault also suggested that the dominant cultural norms in any given epoch are connected to the prevailing morality of that place and time. He argued that there is an implicit set of values associated with every form of knowledge and every mode of understanding. These values have a significant bearing on the people living within that culture and provide the basis of its moral framework. Although this morality may not be explicitly stated, it is woven into the fabric of that societal organization and, to the extent that people are aware of it, is seen as being beyond reproach. In Foucault's analysis, decisions about justice are intertwined with ways of knowing. What is just in the eyes of some may be unjust in those of others. What is moral to members of one group may be immoral to those of another. The proper action to take in a given set of circumstances is related to one's interpretation of morality and justice, which are, in turn, connected to the dominant frames of understanding in that context.[45]

In Foucault's analysis, one of the more significant myths of the modern epoch is that reason and rationality are value-neutral and do not impose a specific moral code on anyone. He pointed out that those who do not subscribe to a modern point of view—where reason and rationality are held in high esteem—are typically faulted for not thinking properly or as failing to work toward what are assumed to be the correct goals. People in this position may be labeled as immoral or insane. What is perceived to be virtuous or evil emerges in relation to the modern perspective, where the distinction between these two provides the basis for judging people and placing them in one category or another. In Foucault's analysis, conventional interpretations of the Enlightenment place restrictions on the kinds of thought and action considered to be acceptable and morally righteous. Modern society, as a result, shuns, constrains, or punishes those who fail to subscribe to them.[46]

Foucault proposed that there is a tension between reason and unreason, invoking Nietzsche's sentiment regarding the dynamic between the Apollonian and the Dionysian. The tendency in the modern era is to support, cherish, and valorize reason while demonizing unreason, pushing the latter into the margins or seeking to eliminate it altogether. The irony of this phenomenon, from Foucault's point of view, is that attempting to repress and contain unreason creates a situation where it can grow in a subterranean way, becoming a much larger phenomenon with the potential to more profoundly influence the social order than it would if it had been accepted and allowed to coexist with reason in the first place.[47]

Foucault also argued that in addition to the dominant discourse having a constraining influence on ideas that do not fit into its ideal framework, there is an ongoing effort in modern society to systematize physical control. Over time, institutions become increasingly effective in guiding people toward serving institutional goals. This involves using sophisticated techniques of observation to monitor individuals and ensure they are behaving in ways that resonate with institutional expectations. He observed this form of "panopticism" emerging surreptitiously and serving to effectively keep people in line with institutional preferences. Developing and enforcing an overarching set of rules, laws, and mores serves to further rationalize the organization of the social order and enforce a comprehensive system of control. Foucault argued that these techniques and practices can be found in prisons, schools, hospitals, and other institutions, facilitating the continued institutional management of individual lives on a broad scale.[48]

Foucault also expressed the view that the sciences have historically played an important role in aiding this process by providing the information and analysis needed to effectively steer people toward institutional objectives. Science can do this in a number of ways, from studying individuals and groups in order to learn more about their beliefs and behaviors to testing and identifying techniques of management in order to see which are likely to be more successful than others. He argued that institutional research and its partner in political advising enable those in power to better understand the situation they are overseeing and decide on the actions they can take to accomplish their goals. The knowledge provided by social scientists can thus serve as an integral component of social engineering, leading to positive incentives for people who behave in ways that are consistent with institutional interests and setting up barriers to obstruct those who do not.[49]

In spite of this assessment, Foucault was not entirely pessimistic. He did not see institutional domination and ideological control as all-encompassing, but argued that even in the midst of this overriding pressure to conform, there continue to be "points of resistance" where people somehow manage to break free of the system and think and act independently of its logic, norms, and traditions. From his point of view, opportunities to develop and maintain alternative perspectives do exist, albeit in a significantly constrained and diminished form.[50]

While Foucault was critical of the modern ethos, he did not reject the ideas of the Enlightenment altogether. He maintained that one of its more valuable contributions to social thought could be found in its emphasis on critique. He argued that independent thought—that which views truth claims from a critical perspective and seeks to develop original and innovative alternatives to the dominant discourse—can serve as a potential pathway to enlightenment. In Foucault's analysis, independent thinking continues to be possible, even in the context of what appears to be the overwhelming influence of institutional domination and control.[51]

JEAN-FRANÇOIS LYOTARD

Another author who contributed to this discussion was the postmodern philosopher Jean-François Lyotard. Lyotard adopted a skeptical attitude toward the possibility of universal truth. He focused on "metanarratives"—the prevailing conceptual frames that exist in society and lead people to understand the world in specific ways. Metanarratives, in Lyotard's view, provide the modes of understanding that legitimate the values and beliefs of a given social order, but also limit the ability of alternative ideas to gain a foothold and make their way into the mainstream.[52]

One metanarrative that has dominated in the Western world is what Lyotard called "the grand narrative" of modernity. This is the story of the Enlightenment that has been salient in the modern era, where scientific and cultural development along with reason and a rationally organized political economy are thought to be leading humanity along the path to a better future. Rather than evaluating the grand narrative in an analytical manner to determine its efficacy relative to other narratives, Lyotard characterized it as a myth that prevailed throughout this time period. From the perspective of people living within the auspices of this myth, it seemed to be the only way to understand the world and live in it. Lyotard suggested that the grand narrative had become so deeply ingrained in Western culture that it served as more than a philosophical perspective. Instead, it had become an unquestioned reality that provided the basis for making sense of experience at the personal and societal levels.[53]

Lyotard observed that the institutions of Western civilization—including those associated with government, business, and education—evolved in relation to this belief system and incorporated its ideas into their burgeoning organizational structure. In this context, laws, mores, and traditions all formed in conjunction with these beliefs and values, developing alongside the material apparatus and providing people with a comprehensive ideological framework for managing their everyday lives.[54]

Lyotard argued that although the grand narrative had become dominant, its influence diminished in the latter half of the twentieth century. He suggested that technological developments and changes in the nature of communication contributed to its ongoing decline and gave way to the emergence of newer, local narratives. In Lyotard's analysis, these smaller narratives more closely resonated with the experiences and ideas of different groups of people making up the larger society. They tended to embody a collection of frames rather than an all-encompassing, unified perspective.[55]

The shift to localized narratives observed by Lyotard coincided with the development of a more culturally diverse social order and provided a wider range of ideas for those whose worldviews did not fit neatly into the logic of the grand narrative. Lyotard characterized this state of affairs as "the postmodern condition," where there was no longer a single way to understand the world, but a variety of perspectives circulating throughout society, each with its own beliefs and practices.[56]

He acknowledged that the challenges arising in conjunction with this trend were formidable, pointing out that when conflicting worldviews clash, there is a tendency for the holders of one perspective to judge others on the basis of their own, familiar way of seeing the world. He saw this habit as misguided in that it presumes the superiority of one's own perspective over others and relies on this perspective as a standard of evaluation in any ideological confrontation. To Lyotard, there is an inherent narrow-mindedness in the assumption that one can assess a particular perspective using the principles of another, and he argued that ways of seeing the world can only be judged on the basis of the standards of the group holding those views.[57]

He understood that conflicting perspectives are often incompatible with one another but suggested that being cognizant of the socially constructed nature of knowledge can help us learn to "tolerate the incommensurable" and make inroads toward intergroup acceptance and mutual respect.[58] Recognizing the potential validity of different perspectives means extending the limits of one's comprehension and seeking to understand others from their point of view. He encouraged the idea of accepting the possibility that another's perspective might have some redeeming qualities, even in the face of what may seem on the surface to be its glaring flaws. Doing this does not mean relinquishing one's own personally held ways of seeing the world, but being open to the possibility that other perspectives may have a degree of insight that cannot be immediately appreciated from one's personal vantage point. This suggests that unfamiliar perspectives might possess elements of value that are not evident when attempting to evaluate them on the basis of one's own trusted but potentially narrow standard of judgment.[59]

In addition, Lyotard argued that although the grand narrative has declined, representatives of established institutions persist in their attempts to preserve its legitimacy, using their influence in government, business, education, religion, and other spheres. This phenomenon is particularly evident at the university level, where the organizational structures in place push scholars, teachers, and researchers to support what are characterized as the only legitimate ideas and goals. In this environment, academics experience considerable pressure to meet the expectations of officialdom and join in the effort to maintain the integrity and prevalence of the grand narrative. Lyotard suggested that this process interferes with the formation of independent analyses and transforms scholarly work from that of open-ended inquiry inspired by intellectual curiosity to officially sanctioned research and teaching managed by established authorities.[60]

While these pressures are not all-encompassing, they have a profound impact on the nature and directions of academic knowledge. In Lyotard's view, this dynamic can lead scholars to be concerned about "performativity," where they are inclined to approach their work in ways that reflect the institutional requirements of their field. A result of this is that their goals are less connected to independent thought and, instead, become centered on meeting the demands of their profession and supporting institutions. Performativity, in this sense, diminishes the potential of scholars to think and act in ways that are free of institutional constraint.[61]

This relates to the social sciences in the sense that the pressure to conform to official expectations and the performativity it engenders can lead researchers to internalize the interests and goals of their home institutions as well as those of government and business. Their inclination to abide by these expectations can limit their range of analysis and diminish their ability to act as leaders in the domain of social thought. Lyotard did not claim that all social scientists succumb to these pressures, but that the pattern of acquiescence is plainly evident for all those who are willing and able to see it.[62]

In sum, Lyotard's position regarding the question of epistemology was one that focused on the growing range of perspectives in contemporary society and the declining presence of a unified worldview. He characterized this transition as part of the ongoing differentiation of ideas and the emergence of new ways to see the world. He did not advocate resisting or redirecting this trend, but encouraged the notion of celebrating difference and recognizing the inherent value in accepting a range of outlooks in academia and in society broadly. In his view, the drift toward the disintegration of the grand narrative and its replacement in the form of multiple, localized narratives was already happening, and this was a trend that should be nurtured and developed further.[63]

RELATIVISM

There are many others who have contributed to the elusive and varied ideas of relativism, but at this point it seems prudent to identify some of its principal features to develop a better sense of its meaning for the sake of our larger discussion. Again, the above authors are not "pure" relativists, but aspects of their work connect at times with this loosely defined set of concepts.

One assertion that emerges consistently in the domain of relativist thought is a tendency to doubt claims of universality that are attached to any single way of seeing the world. We can observe a general skepticism in relativism regarding the notion that some perspectives are inherently superior to others. Ideas that become dominant in a particular context may attract a following of believers who see it as a manifestation of the one and true reality, but this esteemed position can fade over time—or in some cases die out quickly—leaving the door open for alternative ideas, which then take their place as the new leaders of the pack. A relativist position is one that not only doubts the possibility of universal truth but calls into question the endeavor of seeking universal truth in the first place. Modern thinkers involved in the ongoing effort to attain universal truths about the social world are themselves engaged in a dubious quest.[64]

Then what is truth according to relativism? Perhaps the best that can be said from within this orientation is that truth is in the eye of the beholder. That is, if a person or group of people come to believe that they have attained a measure of truth, this is their truth. This is what they believe, and to them, it is the truth. This truth may be connected to a host of other beliefs and serve as the foundation for additional ideas, but regardless of these connections, it is considered to be the truth from their point of view. Knowledge in this sense is fundamentally subjective, meaning it is connected to the individual subject and not necessarily attached to claims of objectivity or universality.

Relativists also seek to expose potential weaknesses in the allegedly neutral assertions of others, particularly those who claim that their position transcends the limitations of any perspective whatsoever. There is a tendency within relativism to question claims that have come to be accepted as truth, and this accompanies a drive to reveal the unstated assertions and hidden biases underlying them. Relativists are disposed to "deconstruct" the validity of truth claims, taking them apart piece by piece to reveal the veiled inconsistencies that may be lurking in the depths of their seemingly impervious outer armor. Doing so can unveil the subjective dimensions of all analyses and conclusions, including those presented as being objective or universal in nature.[65]

A related characteristic of relativism involves questioning the legitimacy in any attempt to construct a hierarchy or ranking of ideas. There tends to be a general acceptance within the relativist camp on this issue that the only way to do this is to select the criteria used to make this determination. This is a normative endeavor and cannot be done in a completely neutral or dispassionate manner. There are many histories, many ways of understanding the social world, and these cannot be definitively evaluated without establishing the standards of judgment involved in doing so.[66]

A fourth characteristic we can observe as being connected to relativism is the contention that marginalized perspectives may be valuable in their own right, but when they do not resonate with the dominant beliefs of the established order, they are denied the opportunity to become more commonly accepted. This is to say that the processes involved in determining which perspectives make it to the top and which do not are inherently connected to the conditions in place in each context. While one does not determine the other, in this analysis, the interplay between the two facilitates the continually changing hierarchy of ideas circulating in society. Relativism thus draws our attention to the uneven playing field in the world of ideas. Since the task of selecting the criteria used to assess the validity of a perspective is arbitrary, those with the power to establish these criteria have a greater potential to determine what can be considered legitimate knowledge. It is, therefore, not the inherent merit of a position that lends it credibility in a given field or in the domain of public consciousness, but the power dynamics, cultural traditions, and normative beliefs of the people in that field and in the larger society that influence this determination.

A fifth point we have observed in the writings of these authors is the assertion that morality is intimately connected to the knowledge framework of an individual or group. In this sense, every form of knowledge has a set of ethical imperatives embedded in it. The promotion of certain ways of thinking and acting throughout society involves the parallel promotion of a concomitant set of ethical beliefs. When dominant institutions support a particular perspective, relativists are inclined to view this as an effort to communicate not only a given form of knowledge but also a statement about what should be thought of as right and wrong. From a relativist point of view, this activity can subtly control people by indirectly imposing a normative belief system and moral code upon them.

The goal of social inquiry from within relativism is less about guiding the ideas of others than it is about considering a range of perspectives and encouraging people to develop their own ideas based on a worldview of their choosing. This implies a shift in the role of the social scientist from that of an enlightened individual seeking to share specific insight or knowledge with others to one who is engaged in an effort to understand social phenomena in an independent manner. A relativist approach transforms social science from a top-down endeavor to one that involves working together with others in an ongoing discussion about possible ways to make sense of what is happening in the social world and being a part of a larger search for meaning in a broader context.

AN EVALUATION OF RELATIVISM

The ideas associated with relativism provide a sharp contrast to those of positivism by drawing attention to the influence of implicit belief systems and institutional power in the formation of knowledge about the social world. Relativism offers a significant challenge to mainstream social science by exposing the perspectival character of social research and showing how the unstated assumptions of investigators can shape the substance of their inquiry. Although this loosely held together set of ideas may have its own shortcomings, the fundamentals of relativism highlight dimensions of social science that many scholars do not wish to acknowledge, namely the socially constructed and culturally normative nature of their analyses and conclusions.

Raising these epistemological issues highlights the point that social scientists always operate in relation to a particular conceptual framework. While most researchers do not subscribe to the ideas of relativism, some have become increasingly focused on the ways their own worldviews may be influencing their work. Relativism encourages social scientists to think about their preconceptions regarding social phenomena and how these may be conditioning their results. Researchers are increasingly inclined to consider the possibility that they might be skipping over key conceptual steps in assessing social issues and drawing on perspectives that are in place because of their proximity to established authority. Relativism has, in this sense, motivated social scientists to critically examine their own practices and take a hard look at their unstated assumptions about the social world generally.

The emphasis of relativism on the subjective dimensions of social scientific knowledge lends a degree of credibility to the notion that there can be more than one valid way to understand a social situation. This raises the idea that different modes of thought can exist on a given topic and that it is possible to simultaneously accept a variety of perspectives as being insightful assessments of the phenomena involved. Even in cases where rigorous methods of research have been employed in an investigation, there can be significant disagreements about how to interpret the data. This points to the prominent role of perspective in social science and in knowledge about the social world generally.

Another related contribution of relativism to the social sciences is its emphasis on the potential legitimacy of ideas outside the boundaries of established thought. Research perspectives continue to diversify over time, due in large part to a growing awareness of the connections between power and knowledge. The emphasis of relativism on the notion that ideas have a better chance of being seen as legitimate when they are connected to established authority raises the possibility that those that do not match conventional analyses may also have something to offer. The realization that institutional power plays such an important role in the formation of knowledge motivates social scientists to be more open to ideas that do not fit neatly into the rubric of mainstream thought.

Although relativism has had this favorable influence on the trajectory of social science, it is subject to some significant drawbacks as well. One of its primary weaknesses is that it embodies an inherent contradiction in terms of its basic assumptions and claims. Specifically, the notion that truth is in the eye of the beholder is problematic in that it can lead one to characterize all knowledge as a matter of personal opinion. Taking relativism to its extreme can give rise to the conclusion that the social world is simply what people make it out to be and that there is no such thing as reality outside of human experience.

A central dilemma of this assertion is that those taking this position are making a truth claim about the nature of knowledge while at the same time arguing that truth is relative. In making these arguments simultaneously, they are saying that they know the truth about knowledge while also saying that truth is what one perceives it to be. This poses a problem for them in the sense that it suggests it is possible to call into question the validity of all universals while at the same proposing a universal claim about the nature of knowledge.

Perhaps the best way to illustrate this point is through a fictitious scenario in a college classroom where the relativist professor stands before the class and says, "The lesson for today is that truth is in the eye of the beholder." Let us imagine for a moment that the students in the classroom dutifully write down this statement with the intent to study it carefully so they will be enlightened about the nature of knowledge and reality in the future. After some thought, one student raises her hand and asks the professor "Will this be on the exam?" The professor replies by saying, "Well, I suppose it might. Why do you ask?" The student then responds in the following way: "I'm wondering if this statement applies to the material we are learning in this class. If it does, then wouldn't that mean that the statement you just made is also potentially fallible, and therefore shouldn't we be open to the possibility that not all truth is in the eye of the beholder? Also, are you saying that there are no truths that are universal? And if you are saying this, does this mean you're making a universal truth claim? And if you are making a universal truth claim, doesn't this contradict the claim that no truths are universal?"

Hopefully, the reader can see where the discussion is going. It highlights the inherent contradictions involved in asserting the position that all truth claims are subjective by calling into question the validity of this truth claim as well, which then largely undermines the substance of the initial point. One who subscribes to this premise is left with the dilemma of having to accept an assertion as true while also taking the position that accepting it undermines its validity. Relativists are prone to implicitly embrace this dual position without acknowledging that the two aspects of it are irreconcilable.

In the face of this contradiction, scholars drawing on the ideas of relativism routinely find themselves in the awkward position of having to express themselves without making overt truth claims. Those taking this position are inclined to write or speak in ways that suggest they are not actually advocating a particular perspective, but alluding to one set of ideas or another without taking a firm stand on any of them. In other words, accepting and promoting the idea that all truth claims are simply constructions leaves relativists with the task of trying to convey ideas without appearing to have them come across as actual truth claims. To the extent that social scientists adopt this course of action, they diminish the potential of the field to offer a significant contribution to intellectual thought in a substantive way. This relegates the social scientist to one who can only present speculative suggestions without being able to definitively clarify the meaning or the substance behind those suggestions.

Another key weakness of relativism is that it deprives social scientists of the ability to assess the quality of competing ideas. Relativists tell us that one can only make such judgments by relying on an arbitrary reference point and, since selecting this point is always a normative endeavor, such a determination is an implicit expression of a particular perspective. While there is certainly some merit to this assertion, taking it to an extreme prevents one from being able to evaluate even the most poorly formed arguments. Embracing the idea that truth is relative leaves scholars empty-handed in their attempt to review analyses of any sort, whether these originate inside or outside academia.

Attempting to put this view into practice reveals its problematic nature. One only needs to briefly reflect on two very distinct statements to demonstrate the contradictory elements of this assertion. The first of these statements might be the following: "There are many different cultures around the world." This position certainly contains a number of normative assumptions—as, for example, regarding the meaning of the word "culture"—but it is nevertheless one that can survive critical scrutiny. The second statement is simply this: "There are no cultural differences among people from around the world." This is a position that is difficult to defend—both on empirical and conceptual grounds—and it illustrates the point that the relativist stance becomes unwieldy when one attempts to cling to it in a dogmatic fashion. The normative nature of the criteria required to compare these two statements does not necessitate the conclusion that one is therefore unable to evaluate them. It is accurate to state that all social scientific analyses rely on a normative conceptual framework, but it is also clear that not all statements are of the same caliber when the standard of judgment is a connection to empirical evidence. It is certainly a choice to include a link to perceived reality as among the criteria used to review social scientific statements, but this is a choice social scientists make consciously on the basis of the principles in their field. The normative foundations of the social sciences do not preclude the possibility of being able to assess the relative validity of one truth claim versus another. In taking the position that any degree of normativity undermines the substance of a truth claim, relativists prevent themselves from being able to appraise even the most basic statements without violating the premises of their own critique. Asserting the position that there are conflicting points of view is not, in itself, contradictory, but moving from this initial premise to the conclusion that no assessment is possible leads one to shy away from refuting any claims whatsoever. Saying that there are many different perspectives and stopping there leaves the door open to the proliferation of ideas that cannot withstand the simplest forms of criticism.

In spite of this issue, relativists continue to challenge the ideas of others, but they are inclined do so in ways that avoid addressing the epistemological contradictions involved. That is, they are not motivated to acknowledge the point that their participation in any evaluative discussion means that they too are drawing on an implicit conceptual foundation. One might think that a true relativist would cease and desist all attempts at analysis on these grounds, but it is clear that most have not taken this route. In engaging in analyses of this sort, they are betraying their own proclamation regarding the problems involved in relying on an arbitrary selection of criteria behind an argument, and this throws them headlong into their own assertions about the normative nature of critique in general.

Authors infusing elements of relativism into their work do write about social issues and often have something valuable to contribute to intellectual discussions on these issues, but they generally use great care to avoid presenting their ideas in an explicit or straightforward way. In these instances, they offer implicit assertions in their writing, requiring a bit of guesswork and decoding on the part of the reader to identify them. When left unchecked, this approach appears to enable authors to have it both ways in the sense that they can criticize the truth claims of others as being grounded in cultural normativity while also communicating their own assertions in an ambiguous and indirect manner.

Taking relativism to its extreme suggests that it is not actually necessary to venture into the field to do research, because whatever one might come back with would still only be conjecture since everything is ultimately a matter of personal perspective. Some authors have gone as far as to suggest that all social research, analyses, and conclusions are only "text" and, as such, are not any more significant or revealing of truth than other assertions.[67] This is an example of the debilitating impact relativism can have on the directions and substance of social science on the whole.

Examining these issues draws our attention to an additional weakness of the relativist position and that is its inability to offer substantive answers to ethical questions. Accepting the idea that there are many forms of knowledge and that there is no way to judge the superiority of one over another leaves relativist authors in a bit of a quandary when it comes to making ethical determinations. The relativist claim that the dominant analyses in the social sciences are socially constructed and grounded in normative processes interferes with their potential to address the topic of ethics in a definitive way, lest they once again fall prey to their own critique. The unavoidable presence of ethics in all social scientific work is, in relativism, a possibility that may or may not be true. Relativists at times try to sidestep ethical commitments altogether and, instead, argue that there are different sets of ethics that vary on the basis of culture and context.

The relativist reluctance to take a stand on ethical issues is ironically similar to the position of the positivists—that ethical considerations have no place in the realm of social science. In the case of the positivists, the overriding belief is that adopting a particular code of ethics interferes with one's neutrality regarding the issues involved. In the case of the relativists, there are no ethical positions that can be said to definitively transcend human judgment, and therefore it is impossible to find an ethical stand that is not in some way culturally normative. In both cases, we see that it is the quest for absolutes that drives their affinity for unfettered neutrality and results in a refusal to overtly embrace an ethical stance. This modus operandi is driven by the belief that relying on one perspective or another diminishes the breadth of one's perception and calls into question the potential validity of one's analyses and conclusions.

Espousing the position that it is not the place of social scientists to allow ethics into the domain of their work leaves both relativists and positivists without the ability to adequately challenge even the most egregious societal offences. One only needs to consider the issue of genocide to make this point. It is not simply the research and teaching of social scientists that is of concern here. It is their willingness to take an ethical stand on important social issues. The analyses and conclusions of social scientists often play a key role in informing the perceptions of political and economic leaders, as well as those in the larger population. When scholars refrain from inserting their own ethical concerns into the mix, they provide new opportunities for unethical individuals to advance their ideas. The work of social scientists is an inherently ethical endeavor, and the relativist and positivist reluctance to overtly embrace a clear ethical stand on the issues they address can have a significant bearing on the subsequent actions of people living in the everyday world and on the directions of society in the long run.

While philosophical relativism has indeed offered significant contributions to social theory and to the social sciences generally, it is also fraught with substantial conceptual weaknesses, and these diminish its ability to provide researchers with effective ways to participate in the task of developing new insight into the social world. It is true that relativism draws attention to the subjective nature of social inquiry and reveals the hidden biases in the prevailing assessments of social phenomena. However, it must also be noted that its failure to offer a feasible way to address these issues gives credence to ideas that oversimplify and obfuscate the substance of knowledge in the scientific world and in society broadly. The tendency of relativist authors to critically evaluate dominant frames can be valuable, but this value is diminished by its inclination toward infinite regress. Although the constructed nature of social scientific work may be an obstacle to the development of any form of transcendent knowledge, this is insufficient justification to refrain from embracing the challenge of seeking to produce enlightening analyses and conclusions, including those that cut through the myths of popular belief and shed new light on important social issues. Social science has the potential to do these things, but only when its practitioners are theoretically informed, empirically grounded, and committed to doing the work needed to move in this direction.

NOTES

1. There is an extensive literature on the ideas of cultural relativism in social science. A significant contribution to this discussion can be found in the work of Clifford Geertz and Michael F. Brown. Please see: Clifford Geertz, "The Impact of the Concept of Culture on the Concept of Man," in *The Interpretation of Cultures* (New York, NY: Basic Books, 1973). Also, please see: Michael F. Brown, "Cultural Relativism 2.0," *Current Anthropology* 49, no. 3 (June 2008): 363–83.

2. Boas outlined this view most extensively in: Franz Boas, *The Mind of Primitive Man* (New York, NY: Macmillan Co., 1911, 1938, 1944), 145–58. He also reaffirms this position in: Franz Boas, *Race, Language, and Culture* (New York, NY: The Macmillan Company, 1940), 199–200.

3. Boas lays out this position in *The Mind of Primitive Man*, 3–18 and 253–72.

4. Boas, *The Mind of Primitive Man*, 253–72.

5. Boas outlined this view in his sole-authored article, "The Study of Geography," *Science* 9, no. 210 (February 11, 1887): 137–41.

6. Michael Brown outlines some of the prevalent analyses of cultural relativism. For a more thorough portrayal of these positions, please see: Brown, "Cultural Relativism 2.0," 363–83.

7. Brown, "Cultural Relativism 2.0," 363–83.

8. Brown, "Cultural Relativism 2.0," 363–83.

9. Brown, "Cultural Relativism 2.0," 363–83.

10. Nietzsche lays out his position on this issue in a number of texts, but he does so most prominently in: Friedrich Nietzsche, *The Genealogy of Morals*, ed. Dr. Oscar Levy, trans. Horace B. Samuel and J. M. Kennedy (Edinburgh and London: T. N. Foulis, 1913).

11. Nietzsche, *The Genealogy of Morals*, 1–35.

12. Nietzsche discusses the master and slave moralities in several of his writings. Please see: Nietzsche, *The Genealogy of Morals*, 35–47. Also see: Friedrich Nietzsche, *Beyond Good and Evil: Prelude to a Philosophy of the Future*, trans. Walter Kaufmann (New York, NY: Vintage Books, 1989; orig. pub. 1886), 204–9.

13. Nietzsche, *The Genealogy of Morals*, 35–47.

14. Nietzsche, *The Genealogy of Morals*, 35–56.

15. Nietzsche, *The Genealogy of Morals*, 27–211.

16. Nietzsche, *The Genealogy of Morals*, 194–98.

17. Nietzsche, *The Genealogy of Morals*, 195.

18. Nietzsche, *The Genealogy of Morals*, 194–206.

19. This is one example of the many where the reader must tease Nietzsche's position out of the text. Please see: Nietzsche, *The Genealogy of Morals*, 154–211.

20. Nietzsche, *The Genealogy of Morals*, 149–51.

21. Nietzsche, *The Genealogy of Morals*, 194–98.

22. Nietzsche, *The Genealogy of Morals*, 194–98.

23. Nietzsche, *Beyond Good and Evil*, 191–211.

24. Friedrich Nietzsche, *The Birth of Tragedy*, trans. Walter Kaufman (New York, NY: Vintage Books, 1967; orig. pub. 1872), 97.

25. Nietzsche, *The Genealogy of Morals*, 208.

26. Nietzsche, *The Genealogy of Morals*, 207–9.

27. Nietzsche, *The Birth of Tragedy*, 35.

28. Nietzsche, *The Birth of Tragedy*, 35.

29. Nietzsche, *The Birth of Tragedy*, 35–37.

30. Nietzsche, *The Birth of Tragedy*, 33–72.

31. Friedrich Nietzsche, *Ecce Homo: How One Becomes What One Is*, trans. Walter Kaufman (New York, NY: Vintage Books, 1969, orig. pub. 1908), 272.

32. Nietzsche, *The Birth of Tragedy*, 33–72.

33. For more on Nietzsche's notion of the will to power, please see: Friedrich Nietzsche, *The Will to Power*, trans. Walter Kaufmann and R. J. Hollingdale, ed. Walter Kaufmann (New York, NY: Vintage, 1967; orig. pub. 1901).

34. We will see in chapter 3 that Hans-Georg Gadamer and other scholars writing in the hermeneutical tradition also use the concept of horizon to denote a particular way of understanding the world.

35. Nietzsche, *Beyond Good and Evil*, 162.

36. Nietzsche, *The Genealogy of Morals*, 119.

37. Nietzsche, *Ecce Homo*, 261.

38. Foucault used the terms "power" and "knowledge" in his analysis, but it seems that when he used the word "knowledge," the meaning is closer to consciousness. For more on his position on this topic, please see: Michel Foucault, *Power/Knowledge: Selected Interviews and Other Writings 1972–1977* (New York, NY: Pantheon Books, 1972).

39. Foucault presents this view of history in the preface of: Michel Foucault, *The Order of Things: An Archaeology of the Human Sciences* (London: Routledge, 2005, orig. pub. 1966), xxii–xxv.

40. Foucault discusses the concept of "episteme" in: *The Order of Things*. Please see, in particular, pages xxiii–xxvi.

41. Foucault, *Power/Knowledge*, 131.

42. Foucault, *Power/Knowledge*, 131.

43. Michele Foucault, *Discipline and Punish: The Birth of the Prison*, trans. Alan Sheridan (New York, NY: Vintage Books, 1995; orig. pub. 1975), 135–69.

44. Foucault, *Power/Knowledge*, 131–33.

45. Foucault, *Power/Knowledge*, 41.

46. Foucault, *Power/Knowledge*, 51.

47. Foucault, *Power/Knowledge*, 51.

48. Foucault, *Discipline and Punish*, 195–228.

49. Foucault makes this connection in the book *Discipline and Punish*. One example of his position on this can be found on pp. 183–92.

50. Foucault mentions this in: Michel Foucault, *The History of Sexuality Volume 1: An Introduction*, trans. Robert Hurley (New York, NY: Pantheon Books, 1978), 95–98.

51. Michel Foucault, "What is Enlightenment," in *The Foucault Reader*, ed. Paul Rabinow (New York, NY: Pantheon Books, 1984), 32–50.

52. Lyotard outlines this position most thoroughly in: Jean-François Lyotard, *The Postmodern Condition: A Report on Knowledge*, trans. Geoff Bennington and Brian Massumi (Minneapolis, MN: University of Minnesota Press, 1984).

53. Lyotard discusses this concept throughout *The Postmodern Condition*, but specific instances can be found in the Introduction, pp. xxiii–xxv, and on pages 37–41.

54. Lyotard, *The Postmodern Condition*, xxiii–xxv.

55. Lyotard, *The Postmodern Condition*, 36–41.

56. Lyotard, *The Postmodern Condition*, 60.

57. Lyotard, *The Postmodern Condition*, 60–67.

58. Lyotard, *The Postmodern Condition*, xxv.

59. Lyotard, *The Postmodern Condition*, 60–67.

60. Lyotard, *The Postmodern Condition*, 60–67.

61. Lyotard, *The Postmodern Condition*, 41–52.

62. Lyotard, *The Postmodern Condition*, 23–52.

63. Lyotard, *The Postmodern Condition*, 60–67.

64. For more on this, please see: Joseph Margolis, *The Truth About Relativism* (Oxford, UK: Blackwell, 1991).

65. For more on deconstruction, please see: Jacques Derrida, *Positions* (Chicago, IL: University of Chicago Press, 1982).

66. One author who presents this view very clearly is Richard Rorty. Please see: Richard Rorty, *Contingency, Irony, and Solidarity* (Cambridge: Cambridge University Press, 1989).

67. Please see: Jacques Derrida, *Of Grammatology*, trans. Gayatri Chakravorty Spivak (Paris: Les Editions de Minuit, 1967).

Chapter 3

Interpretivism

Finding Meaning in Everyday Life

Studying positivism and relativism from a critical point of view has given us food for thought in our effort to identify the characteristics of a balanced epistemological orientation for the social sciences. The first major revelation of this inquiry is that even researchers who are critical of the positivist orientation seek to learn more about people in their social worlds. While these critics may not accept the logic or methodological approaches of the positivist tradition, they are nevertheless inclined to implicitly embrace its emphasis on working to develop new levels of insight into the often unclear and varying dimensions of everyday life. In this sense, elements of the positivist spirit live on, even among its most ardent critics.

The second important point we have encountered thus far is that every social scientific investigation is connected to a theoretical perspective. We have seen that researchers may shift their perspective during the course of a study and that this enables them to form more open-ended and nuanced understandings of their subject matter, but we have also learned that this does not alter the fact that their cultural framework, unstated assumptions, and systems of classification continue to influence the kinds of data they gather, the organization of their analyses, and the substance of their conclusions.

The important lesson to take away from this discussion is that high-caliber social inquiry requires researchers to be cognizant of the ways their own worldviews may be influencing the projects they are pursuing. There is no getting around the connection between theory and research, and this is why it is crucial for social scientists to be aware of their own ways of making sense of the world rather than succumbing to the illusion that they have none.

The third point emerging in conjunction with our assessment thus far is that even though all social scientific investigations are connected to a particular conceptual framework, this connection does not diminish their potential to generate innovative and insightful conclusions. Social research does not transcend the limits of perspective, but it can nevertheless provide a valuable way to learn about the social world.

Having addressed these preliminary issues, we can now move on to examine the interpretive orientation and its practices. Interpretivism has had a long history and has undergone many permutations over the course of its evolution. It is not limited to a single set of ideas, but embodies an extensive array of points and counterpoints, each providing something unique and vital to its development. To understand the basic characteristics of interpretivism, we begin by identifying some of its underlying principles and show how these have helped transform it into a viable epistemological orientation for the social sciences.

HERMENEUTICS

One of the salient traditions informing interpretivism is the field of hermeneutics. Hermeneutics is an area of study originating in the interpretation of written texts, where scholars seek to decipher the meanings embedded in various passages of religious and philosophical documents. This mode of inquiry expanded over time to include not only written texts but also the interpretation of human social life, with a focus on the importance in understanding the meanings people bring to their actions and the relationships between these meanings and the contexts in which they develop.[1]

William Dilthey was one of the more influential scholars who helped build the conceptual foundation of hermeneutics. Dilthey was a philosopher and psychologist writing in the late 1800s and early 1900s. He characterized hermeneutics as a set of ideas that challenged the dominant epistemological orientation of mainstream social science. Dilthey questioned the notion of relying on the logic of the natural sciences as a means of examining the social world and argued that human social life involves reflection and imagination and is, at its core, intensely personal. He suggested that hermeneutics could serve as a more subtle and empathetic way to study social phenomena in that it goes beyond the practice of observing human behavior and seeks to understand people from their own point of view.[2]

Operating within the framework of hermeneutics means striving to learn about individuals on a personal level—including their beliefs and values—so that their worldviews can become more apparent to the observer. Dilthey proposed that the meanings people hold dear in their lives are central to their sense of self and their perceptions of others, and this is why they are so integral to the social sciences.[3]

In order to work toward a deeper understanding of meaning, Dilthey raised the idea of the hermeneutic circle, where the goal is to consider the relationship between individuals' personal lives and their cultural surroundings. He stressed the need to study the ways the more intimate aspects of meaning are connected to the larger social context and, conversely, how the broader social milieu relates to individual consciousness. Dilthey sought to draw attention to the interplay between these two rather than seeing one as having a unidirectional influence on the other.[4]

The significance of the concept of the hermeneutic circle in the social sciences is that it highlights the context-specific nature of meaning. One of the prevailing arguments in hermeneutics is that it is problematic for social scientists to believe they can isolate and extract such things as the values of individuals from the situational factors in which they are embedded. Studying the personal dimensions of everyday life out of context can lead researchers to misunderstand or mischaracterize them. These more intimate aspects of a person's life can only be understood in terms of their connections to the prevailing norms and traditions of the cultural milieu in which they are situated.[5]

The link between the personal and the social emphasized in hermeneutics can be seen most clearly in the area of communication. Language, in hermeneutics, is more than simply a means of expressing ideas. It provides the conceptual framework through which people's worldviews are constructed and maintained. The origins of hermeneutics in textual analysis led to its focus on the meaning of words, the ways words are put together, and the context of their creation. From a hermeneutical standpoint, these all play a significant role in shaping the ideas involved. Linguists are particularly familiar with this phenomenon as they routinely observe the conceptual differences embedded in the structure of language from one culture to the next. Hermeneutical scholars point out that perspective is so intrinsically connected to language that people who have developed ways of seeing the world in relation to their home language typically do not recognize the colloquial nature of their understanding. It is only when they are faced with a notably different way of seeing the world that the culturally specific nature of their conceptual apparatus becomes apparent.[6]

This point is relevant to the social sciences in that it draws attention to the ways social researchers rely on language as a component of their perspective and the bearing this connection has on their choices about what topics to study, how to frame those topics, and how to convey their findings. This observation raises the question of how researchers can claim to be operating at a level that transcends everyday understanding when their work is bound to the linguistic formations inherent in their home culture and in the terminology used in their respective fields. Hermeneutical scholars emphasize this point to call for a reconceptualization of the social sciences generally—from one claiming to operate at an objective level to one that is admittedly embedded in a specific cultural framework.[7]

This leads us to consider the emphasis of hermeneutics on the connections between knowledge and human interests. In hermeneutics, there are always particular interests surrounding the formation of new knowledge, and these are influential in shaping what people come to see as valid in their assessments of the world around them. This idea is not difficult to understand when examining the different casuistries people develop in their attempt to establish and confirm what they perceive to be true. Clear consistencies exist in terms of the accepted knowledge patterns from one group to the next, and these are connected to the interests people have in each context.[8]

What is perhaps less palatable to the scientific mind is the notion that social scientists themselves are situated in specific contextual settings and have interests and concerns that influence the ways they understand the world and the people they study. Hermeneutical scholars propose that contextual factors surrounding social scientists in their personal and professional lives play a significant role in shaping the kinds of ideas they come to take for granted, how they understand their topics, the ways they approach their work, and the frames they use to make sense of their findings. Social scientists are, thus, not exempt from the influence of situational factors—including their interests, concerns, and perspectives—in shaping how they come to understand the world and go about the task of creating new knowledge.[9]

The next and perhaps most surprising contribution of hermeneutics is the argument that not all tradition has a negative influence in the realm of ideas. In hermeneutics, although traditional frames of understanding may lead social scientists to view the world in a particular way, these perspectives also provide an initial foundation of understanding that can serve as a guide in social research. Social scientists all have personal histories that inform their choices about what they see as important and why they have chosen to engage in their specific areas of research. Their own backgrounds and perspectives lead them to their profession and supply them with the motivation to learn more about the topics of their choosing. Experience, in this sense, can be an important catalyst for social research and provide a crucial function in the development of new ideas.[10]

The point hermeneutic scholars emphasize in this regard is that while one's background is helpful in providing a starting framework for research, it is also important for social scientists to avoid falling into the trap of clinging to their own worldviews in a dogmatic or ideological fashion. One of the more difficult challenges facing social scientists is the requirement that they think about their own potential narrow-mindedness and consider ways to enhance their understandings of the people they are studying. The difficulty arises when scholars are faced with the prospect of having to develop an awareness of the internal contradictions or other weaknesses in their own modes of thought and must shift their perception to broaden their horizons.[11]

At the same time, there is some doubt in the field of hermeneutics regarding the potential of researchers to completely escape the confines of their own conceptual framework, especially since this is grounded in the personal experiences, language, education, and cultural traditions of their home milieu. Hermeneutic scholars argue that it is possible for social scientists to expand their perspectives, provided they make an effort to develop a sense of what these perspectives are in the first place and how these might be limited or in need of expanding. The goal is for researchers to develop a sense of their own "effective-historical consciousness" as a way to better understand how this provides the foundation for what they consider to be valid knowledge and actual truth.[12]

Hermeneutical scholars argue that social scientists are better able to expand their consciousness through a "fusion of horizons."[13] When people develop an awareness of their own worldview and its relationship to their past and present experiences, they can be more open to accepting the potential validity of perspectives other than their own. Being willing and able to reflect on new ideas and weave them into one's existing perceptions of the world is, in the hermeneutical tradition, an example of fusing horizons with another. This is a central goal of hermeneutics and of the interpretive orientation broadly.[14]

It is important to point out that, when applying this idea to social science, hermeneutic scholars do not characterize it as achieving objectivity or as building a transcendent form of knowledge, but as developing an insightful understanding of the topic one is studying and of the social world generally. This may seem on the surface to be a semantic difference, but from a hermeneutical point of view, there is a legitimate distinction between these two conceptions of truth. Saying that one can achieve objectivity assumes the possibility of being able to escape the limitations of a horizon altogether. The problem with this assumption is that it ignores the ways knowledge of the social world is connected to a particular worldview. All social scientific research and its associate findings, analyses, and conclusions are tied to the horizon through which they are constructed and maintained. What social researchers perceive to be truth is always grounded in a set of assumptions and conceptual categories that enable that truth to exist in the first place. The goal of fusing one's horizon with that of another is to develop new ways of making sense of the world that can carry the holder beyond the realm of unconsciously relying on what may be a limited perspective.[15]

Perhaps the best way to clarify this distinction is to think of the differences between knowledge as factual information and knowledge as understanding. While the first is certainly important and can serve the function of gathering the requisite information about a given situation, knowledge of the facts alone can be limiting in the sense that it does not do much to provide one with a way to make sense of those facts. Achieving a deeper level of understanding means forming new interpretations of a situation and bringing new meaning to a set of facts that might otherwise seem disjointed. Fusing one's horizon with that of another is a way to develop broad understandings of a particular phenomenon and its relationship to the larger social whole.[16]

We can see that hermeneutics has contributed a great deal to the interpretive orientation generally. Its emphasis on meaning and the socially constructed nature of knowledge provides a path for social scientists to approach their work in insightful and theoretically informed ways.

MAX WEBER

Max Weber's ideas also offer a significant contribution to interpretivism through his writings on the philosophy of social science. Although Weber's work is centered in the field of sociology, he devoted a great deal of attention to history, religion, law, politics, and economics, and engaged in the study of regions around the world in China, India, and the United States.[17]

In order to understand Weber's contributions in this area, it is important to begin with a discussion of his concerns regarding the rationalization of society and the consequences of this trend in terms of individual freedom. Weber observed that large-scale institutions in a variety of historical contexts tend to display the pattern of becoming increasingly controlling over the lives of individuals. He was particularly concerned about bureaucracy as a form of institutional organization due to its extraordinarily rational approach to managing people. He saw bureaucracy as one of the most effective forms of societal management, but also as a system that left little room for individual autonomy, where people could live their lives in a free and fulfilled manner as human beings. Weber argued that bureaucracies tend to trap individuals in what he referred to as "a casing as hard as steel," where their own wants, needs, and desires consistently yield to institutional requirements. He took the position that studying the history of civilizations reveals the important point that once bureaucracy becomes the dominant form of organization in a given society, it remains in place until that society collapses altogether.[18]

Weber saw bureaucracy as one example of the larger process of rationalization taking place in modern society. He understood that this trend was an inherent feature of the modern era and did not expect a change in the direction and goals of institutions, but he argued that the ongoing tendency to rationalize all forms of societal organization ironically contributes to a growing irrationality in terms of its consequences. In Weber's analysis, as the structure of society moves in the direction of instrumental rationality in its official organization, the result is a growing absurdity regarding the actual lives of the people living within the confines of that society.[19]

Weber's concern in this regard informed the kind of social science he advocated throughout his lifetime. In particular, he held the view that social scientists have a responsibility to avoid contributing to the further dehumanization of social life. Rather than seeing the primary purpose of social science as uncritically working with institutions to facilitate their objectives—whatever these may be—Weber proposed the idea that social scientists strive for a more informed and enlightened set of goals, including those designed to serve the broader interests of human beings generally. He hoped this would be a guiding principle for them as they engaged in research, teaching, and advising.[20]

Weber suggested that social scientists seek to develop an awareness of their surroundings and consider the potential consequences of the choices they make in deciding what to study, how to frame their topics, and interpret their findings. He believed that being mindful of the ways social research may be used to further rationalize the institutional order constituted an important starting point in deciding how to proceed as a social scientist. Rather than turn a blind eye to this trend in their work, social scientists should acknowledge it and avoid the trap of inadvertently contributing to the steel casing of civilization and its burgeoning limits to individual freedom.[21]

This perspective led Weber to seek alternatives to a view of society as a machine that could be engineered in a mechanistic way to help it run more smoothly. He developed a strong aversion toward the notion of approaching social research in a matter-of-fact or purely dispassionate manner. In particular, he rejected the idea that social scientific analyses can be reduced to simple cause-and-effect relationships, where one aspect of the social order is seen as having a direct and all-encompassing influence on another. As an alternative, he focused on the interactive nature of everyday life and studied the ties between historically specific settings and the norms and traditions emerging in particular contexts. His epistemological approach involved looking at the connections between personal beliefs, institutional arrangements, and large-scale social patterns in the attempt to better understand how these intersected with one another. Weber introduced an integrative way to bring together seemingly disparate domains—the personal worlds of consciousness and culture, on the one hand, and the broader, bureaucratic worlds of politics and economy, on the other.[22]

An example of this can be found in his account of the relationship between the Protestant ethic and the spirit of capitalism in the United States. In his study of the New England Calvinist Protestants, Weber observed that these two aspects of the social order displayed what he characterized as an "elective affinity" where each strengthened the other and led to their mutual growth and development. Working toward an informed analysis of this relationship meant developing a sense of the intimate and personal dimensions of human social life while also paying attention to the societal forces involved.[23]

To this end, Weber focused on the concept of *Verstehen* to refer to the idea of seeking to understand people in their own social environments and from their own point of view. He argued that a central task of social science involved developing insight into the ways people see the world and how these perspectives relate to their choices about how to act in it. In Weber's analysis, observing people's behavior is important, but it is only part of the equation. The larger goal of social science extends beyond this and into the domain of meaning—including the effort to learn more about where this behavior is coming from, what motivates it, and what guides it. Weber recognized the limitations in attempting to understand the consciousness of others, but he nevertheless saw it is an integral component of social research.[24]

At the same time, Weber maintained the position that social scientists have a responsibility to approach their work in a value-free manner. This point has been a source of tension among Weberian scholars from the time of his writing to the present. Some, for instance, are inclined to point to Weber's appeal for value-free social science as an indication of the positivist dimensions of his epistemology, while others counter that his emphasis on *Verstehen* and the importance in seeking to understand the meaning of people's actions is evidence of his interpretivist leanings.[25]

To address this disagreement, we can view Weber's appeal to value freedom in the context of the distinctions he drew between the ethics of politics on the one hand and those of social science on the other. In his writings on these two spheres, he sought to challenge the practices of his colleagues whom he observed engaging in research, writing, and teaching from the perspective of a partisan political agenda—all the while presenting their work as though it were purely scientific in nature. Weber argued that much of this activity reflected a desire to advance predetermined political goals that were neatly packaged to give the appearance of being value-neutral. He argued that high-caliber social scientific analyses are those that do not seek to advance a narrow political agenda, but embody an interest in developing a broadly constructed and insightful assessment of the topic at hand. He advocated the position that when research is carried out with specific political goals in mind, the result is likely to convey a limited view of the issues involved and is therefore outside the domain of science. In this sense, social scientists have a responsibility to minimize the extent to which they draw on their own political preferences and, instead, take every measure possible to avoid diminishing the perspicacity of their analyses. Their task is to strive toward a level of value freedom that expands the scope of their work and share this newfound insight with others.[26]

Embedded in this assertion is Weber's acknowledgment that researchers cannot achieve absolute objectivity in their research. He embraced the position that social science always involves some degree of value—including, for instance, the notion that working toward a deeper understanding of the social world is a worthwhile goal. Weber saw the primary aim of social research as one that entails a willingness and ability on the part of researchers to limit their own values and avoid constructing a prescriptive image of the aspects of the social world they are studying. He did not expect, nor did he advocate, an infallible approach to social inquiry, but one that involved minimizing the researcher's values as much as possible in an effort to develop a more comprehensive understanding of the social phenomena being studied.[27]

Weber's contributions to interpretivism can thus be identified as a call to find a balance between the quest for broad knowledge and the recognition that empirical inquiries are always connected to an underlying conceptual framework. He hoped that an awareness of the ways larger societal processes relate to interpersonal and culturally normative beliefs would provide fertile ground for the development of innovative ideas and investigative practices, ultimately building a more subtle and enlightening epistemological foundation for social research.[28]

PHENOMENOLOGY—EDMUND HUSSERL

Another key thinker whose writings provided a significant contribution to the interpretive orientation is Edmund Husserl. Husserl was a European philosopher writing in the early part of the twentieth century on questions regarding human consciousness and perception. He developed the philosophy of phenomenology, focusing on the ways people experienced social phenomena internally. One of his central interests was exploring the relationship of these experiences to their overall worldviews and their choices about how to interact with others. He sought to construct an epistemological framework that helped facilitate inquiry into the realm of personal experience and better understand it from an interpretive point of view.[29]

In phenomenology, the word "phenomenon" has a particular meaning originating in the Greek *phainomenon*, or "that which appears or is seen." We can think of phenomenology as the study of appearances—specifically, how people perceive the experiences they encounter in their personal lives. This draws attention to the subjective dimensions of experience and the ways people understand the world from their own perspective. Husserl argued that experiences are not only external to the individual but can also be internal, such as those associated with feelings, imagination, and dreams. He suggested that these embodied experiences can be as significant as the external variety from the perspective of the person experiencing them, and he drew parallels between the two to show how they relate to one another. He did not suggest that there was a clear distinction between the internal and the external, but rather a continuum where some experiences have elements of both. Husserl maintained that when experience emanates from an external source, the experiencer has a particular viewpoint relative to the experience itself. Applying this to our own example—let us say a person looking at a waterfall—we can easily understand that individuals have the ability to shift their physical position relative to the source and can therefore facilitate different experiences. One may, for instance, choose to go under the waterfall or even in it, allowing the water to fall down from above, thereby changing the nature of that experience. Husserl argued that this kind of shift is also possible in the realm of internal experience, where individuals have the potential to alter their perspective relative to that experience. People having internal embodied experiences do so from a certain standpoint and can shift this to change the nature of that experience for them as well. To the extent that individuals reorient themselves internally, they can create a new sense of that experience and perceive it differently.[30]

This way of understanding experience—as existing in relation to a particular perspective—provides a valuable contribution to interpretivism by drawing attention to the constructed nature of consciousness. On the basis of this idea, we can readily grasp the argument that developing knowledge about the social world is more than passively receiving external stimuli or factual information, but involves adopting a specific frame of mind that enables individuals to make sense of their experiences and understand them in meaningful ways.

Husserl also developed the concept of "intentionality" as an integral component of phenomenology and of interpretivism broadly. The meaning of this term in this context is a bit different from the conventional usage of it in that it is less about the intended goal of a particular physical action than it is about reaching out and extending one's perspective to encounter something different from the original experience. In this sense, intentionality is a deliberate attempt to broaden one's consciousness in order to find meaning in an experience or set of experiences. It is an effort to conceptualize these experiences in a guided fashion, so they can be understood in new ways and from new perspectives. Husserl suggested that this can only be done by extending one's consciousness from where it is in any given moment.[31]

The concept of intentionality is also significant to the interpretive orientation in that it highlights the perspectival nature of knowledge and the range of viewpoints possible in everyday understanding. This idea provides the basis for an approach to social research that seeks insight into the social world as it appears to people from their own perspective. It is markedly different from the practices of positivist social science where the goal is to learn about the objective reality taking place. An implicit assumption of the positivist approach is that the subjectivities of individual perception may cloud one's understanding of the actual reality occurring in a given context. In the domain of phenomenology, however, the goal is to try to understand everyday subjectivities and develop a sense of the appearances people perceive in their personal lives and the meanings they attach to those appearances.

This leads to another key contribution of Husserl to the interpretive orientation and the social sciences generally—and that is the concept of the lifeworld. Husserl depicted the lifeworld as that which people experience in their personal lives and in relation to others. It is the realm of interpersonal interaction and internal reflection and is intimately connected to consciousness and one's sense of perception. The lifeworld, in Husserl's analysis, is something the individual feels is intuitively valid and self-evident. It is the essence of reality from that person's point of view. He referred to this subjective experience as "the thing itself" and characterized it as self-evident from the perspective of the person having the experience.[32]

> The lifeworld is a realm of original self-evidences. That which is self-evidently given is, in perception, experienced as "the thing itself," in immediate presence, or, in memory, remembered as the thing itself; and every other manner of intuition is a presentification of the thing itself. Every mediate cognition belonging in this sphere—broadly speaking, every manner of induction—has the sense of an induction of something intuitable, something possibly perceivable as the thing itself or rememberable as having-been-perceived, etc.[33]

A key component of the lifeworld, in Husserl's analysis, is what he referred to as "the natural attitude." This is a mode of understanding people employ in their everyday lives. It comes about through the experience of living life, interacting with others, and reflecting on the meaning of this experience from a personal perspective. Husserl argued that the natural attitude is a necessary part of social interaction because it provides a way to attribute meaning to one's experience. In framing experience, it brings some degree of perceptible order to one's surroundings and helps individuals understand the world around them. It provides them with a sense of what to expect from others and a way to interact in relation to those expectations. The natural attitude is the conceptual framework people rely on to comprehend their experiences and live their lives on a day-to-day basis.[34]

Husserl argued that the ongoing interplay between the self and others in one's milieu conditions a person's consciousness in ways that tend to be limiting. While the natural attitude provides a consistent frame of understanding of the world for the individual, it is also restrictive in that it coincides with the prevailing set of norms and traditions of that person's home culture. He characterized the natural attitude as being burdened by the influence of one's environment and as having a constraining influence on perception. While people's everyday consciousness is limited, these constraints are typically unnoticed, leading individuals to believe they are experiencing the one and only true reality as it exists around them. In this sense, people are inclined to believe that the meaning they have constructed to understand their experience reflects the full extent of what is possible and is representative of the absolute truth.[35]

Husserl observed that the prevailing goal of mainstream social science is for researchers to adopt a dispassionate approach to their inquiries so they can engage in the endeavor of social research in a neutral manner. He understood the reasoning behind this line of thinking, but argued that social scientific thought tends to be grounded in the logic and ways of understanding that are characteristic of the natural attitude. He maintained that while the ethos of social science heralds the notion of extending one's knowledge beyond the realm of everyday experience, the practices of researchers generally entail drawing on their own culturally normative perspectives as a grounding for their analyses and conclusions. He argued that in instances where new evidence emerges and current scientific conclusions are called into question, the opportunity arises for scholars to bring about a transition to innovative ways of making sense of empirical observations. When these openings occur, however, a common tendency of the purveyors of both the older and newer scientific formulations is to draw on frames of reference borrowed from the natural attitude as a grounding for their positions. This means that while social scientists may believe they are developing original theoretical formulations, they are actually carrying forward preexisting conceptions of the social world that are common in their milieu and employing these as the foundation for their new analyses. The result is that taken-for-granted ways of making sense of the world spill over into social scientific formulations, extending the assumptions embedded in the natural attitude of the researchers themselves. This leads to an unconscious reproducing of the habits of thought in a particular culture, framed in a way that gives the appearance of having transcended the subjective understandings of everyday life.[36]

Husserl suggested that phenomenology and its emphasis on investigating the interpretive dimensions of the social world can serve as a way to address this issue. Rather than characterizing the task of social science as transcending the personal aspects of everyday experience, he proposed the idea of seeking to develop insight into these subjectivities to learn more about how people see themselves and their social environments and striving to understanding the meanings they bring to their actions. The goal of social research then shifts from discovering what is believed to be objective reality to studying the appearances of the social world as experienced by those doing the perceiving.[37]

Husserl contended that in order to properly engage in this area of inquiry, researchers must develop an awareness of the ways they are drawing on the natural attitude and make an effort to bracket this perspective to better understand the subjective nature of their experiences. Engaging in this endeavor requires a living, breathing human being—one who is capable of empathy and genuinely interested in understanding the consciousness of others while also being aware of the potential influence of the natural attitude as misleadingly representing the only possible one and true reality. Husserl suggested that taking this approach can serve as a way to study human consciousness without succumbing to the limitations of the natural attitude or the conceptual weaknesses of positivist social science.[38]

Phenomenology, in Husserl's analysis, provides an appropriate starting point for the social sciences. Its exploration into the domain of appearances offers a way to understand the meaning of personal experience from the standpoint of those having the experience. It does not presume the possibility of transforming this insight into universal abstract laws or an allegedly objective depiction of reality. Instead, Husserl characterized phenomenology as a way to get to the heart of what is most important in the endeavor of social science—the meaning behind one's actions from the actor's point of view.[39]

PHENOMENOLOGY—ALFRED SCHÜTZ

Alfred Schütz also helped advance the philosophy of phenomenology and the interpretive orientation. Schütz infused his ideas into the conceptual framework of phenomenology to further develop the goal of seeking to understand the world as it appears to people from their own perspective. One major contribution of Schütz in this regard is his emphasis on the temporal nature of experience, where elements of the past, present, and future intersect with one another and connect with a person's consciousness over time. Husserl initially introduced the notion of temporality as it relates to consciousness, but Schütz expanded this concept, describing what he characterized as the stream of experience that people encounter in their everyday lives.[40] Schütz saw experience as occurring in the form of a continuous flow, where interpretations of the past can have a bearing on one's understanding of the present and sense of the future. In his analysis, while individuals perceive certain experiences to be significant, they may view other instances as inconsequential or nonsensical based on their perceptions of them at the time. He hypothesized that one's consciousness plays an important role in this deliberative process and can serve as a guide in shaping how a person attributes meaning to a particular moment within the stream of experience. Schütz suggested that meaningful experience can, in turn, have an impact on a person's consciousness. He observed an ongoing interplay between consciousness and experience, where each has the ability to influence the other. The connections between these two are part of an interaction that occurs throughout people's lives, defining how they come to see the world and facilitating the search for meaning along the way.[41]

An example of this phenomenon can be found in the experience of a person hearing a particular piece of music while in the midst of a romantic relationship. This experience may lead that person to develop a unique set of emotions associated with that music. Hearing the same piece years later in a different context may invoke these earlier emotions and foster an experience in the present that has significant meaning to the individual in this newer context. Such an experience may be entirely different from that of another person hearing the same piece, even though both individuals may be listening to it in the same place and at the same time. Schütz's claim is that a person's consciousness—including past memories—can be influential in shaping the ways one interprets and finds meaning in an experience taking place in the present.[42]

In addition, Schütz contended that meaningful experiences of the past can have a bearing on one's expectations regarding the long-term trajectory of their lives. People draw on their interpretations of earlier experiences and the framework of their existing consciousness to develop a sense of their hopes for the future. Their actions in the present can thus be influenced by their sense of the past and provide a conceptual foundation for what they desire and what they believe lies ahead. In Schütz's analysis, perceptions of the past, present, and future are all interwoven in people's consciousness and inform the choices they make every day.[43]

This leads us to the point raised by Schütz regarding the nexus between consciousness, meaning, and action. He maintained that people do not simply act in a predetermined way, based on the conditions in place in a particular setting, but rely on their experiences and the meanings they attribute to those experiences over time as the basis for their choices. Action is, thus, understood as something that occurs in relation to one's perceptions, motivations, and expectations. Human behavior, in Schütz's analysis, is not determined by social forces, but emerges in connection to this ongoing interplay.[44]

Schütz argued that not all actions are planned in a self-conscious manner, where people always make mindful and well-thought-out decisions. In his view, actions can range from being deliberate to those that are spontaneous and carried out reactively, without any planning at all. In this sense, individual consciousness is not directly responsible for all human action, but emotions and bodily reflex can also play a key part in leading a person to engage in one set of behaviors over another.[45]

As in the case of Husserl, Schütz applied this analysis to the consciousness and motivations of social scientists themselves, proposing that members of this group are not exempt from the human dimensions of personal belief, emotion, and social expectation. Schütz maintained that social scientists are integrated into a particular societal fabric, and their consciousness, feelings, and behavior, while not determined by these factors, are nevertheless connected to them in myriad ways. He drew attention to the ties between the milieu of social scientists and the modes of thought that dominate their profession. Specific ways of thinking and communicating inform the frames of knowledge employed by social scientists as they observe and analyze various aspects of the social world they are studying.[46]

This informs Schütz's view of social science generally in that it draws attention to the manner in which researchers see the world around them and make sense of it in relation to their own perspective. He pointed out that social scientists are inclined to approach their work using theories and methods that lead them to convince themselves that they are operating at a level that transcends the conceptual limitations of everyday consciousness. In Schütz's assessment, however, the quest for objectivity facilitates a tendency among social scientists to focus on people's external behavior since this is a component of social life that can be observed directly, without delving into the murky and unverifiable world of personal subjectivities. He challenged the logic of this approach, arguing that all types of social research are grounded in a particular perspective used by social scientists to make sense of their subject matter and form their analyses and conclusions. He maintained that the task of engaging in social research requires investigators to rely on their own consciousness and collection of experiences to decipher the actions of the people they are trying to understand.

To be sure, those scientists admit that phenomena such as nation, government, market, price, religion, art, science refer to activities of other intelligent human beings for whom they constitute the world of their social life; they admit furthermore that alter egos have created this world by their activities and that they orient their further activities to its existence. Nevertheless, so they pretend, we are not obliged to go back to the subjective activities of those alter egos and to their correlates in their minds in order to give a description and explanation of the facts of this social world. Social scientists, they contend, may and should restrict themselves to telling what this world means to them, neglecting what it means to the actors within this social world. Let us collect the facts of this social world, as our scientific experience may present them in a reliable form, let us describe and analyze these facts, let us group them under pertinent categories and study the regularities in their shape and development which then will emerge, and we shall arrive at a system of the social sciences, discovering the basic principles and the analytical laws of the social world. Having once reached this point, the social sciences may confidently leave the subjective analyses to psychologists, philosophers, metaphysicists, or whatever else you like to call idle people bothering with such problems. And, the defender of such a position may add, is it not this scientific ideal which the most advanced social sciences are about to realize? Look at modern economics! The great progress of this science dates exactly from the decision of some advanced spirits to study curves of demand and supply and to discuss equations of prices and costs instead of striving hard and in vain to penetrate the mystery of subjective wants and subjective values.[47]

Schütz contended that researchers cannot engage in social inquiry without drawing on their own perceptions of the phenomena they are studying. He referred to Husserl's claim that although social scientists may believe they are operating objectively, their practices necessarily involve relying on their own experiences in the lifeworld and on the natural attitude as a way to investigate their subject matter and pass on their findings to others. Schütz added that, in spite of these practices, social scientists continue to convince themselves that they are gathering knowledge of the social world that transcends everyday perceptions of reality.[48]

In sum, Schütz's contribution to the development of phenomenology and the interpretive orientation can be seen in his focus on the realm of consciousness and the ways the social world appears to people. This includes how they think about their experiences and the connections of these thought processes to the choices they make in interacting with others in their social environments. His input into this discussion emphasizes not only the importance in studying the phenomena of everyday life as experienced by those living in it but also the perspectives and methods used by social scientists as integral aspects of their research. Perception and action are principal components of the interpretive orientation and underscore its attention to the challenging issue of trying to understand why people do what they do. Schütz ventured into this territory to help social scientists enhance their insight into the ways consciousness relates to the social world and its ties to human behavior.[49]

We can see from this brief review of phenomenology that it has informed the interpretive orientation by providing creative ways to conceptualize the connections between experience, meaning, and action and by highlighting the importance in understanding people on their own terms and from their own point of view. The ideas of these authors in the area of epistemology and in matters of social research serve to strengthen the theoretical foundation of interpretivism and provide new insight into the endeavor of social science as a whole.

The focus of phenomenology on the more ethereal dimensions of consciousness is something that positivists are inclined to characterize as outside the domain of social science, due in large part to the challenges involved in assessing the perspectives of others in a neutral manner. The response of phenomenologists to this critique is that the interpretive nature of human experience does not necessarily render social scientists incapable of understanding that experience. In phenomenology, perspective and experience are at the core of human social life, and studying these as thoroughly as possible is a central task of social research.

INTERPRETIVISM

Our discussion thus far has shed some light on the foundations of interpretivism. Drawing on the work of these scholars, we can begin to develop a sense of the main characteristics of this orientation. We have seen that one of its defining qualities is an emphasis on the meanings people bring to their actions in everyday life. Engaging in research from this vantage point involves observing behavior, but it also entails venturing into the domain of perception to work toward the goal of understanding people on their own terms and in their own milieu. Interpretive social scientists seek not only to learn about what people are doing in their lives, but why they are doing it and what it means from the perspectives of the actors themselves.

Alongside this fundamental starting point is the interpretivist assertion that people conceptualize the world in a variety of ways and that these images are influential in shaping how they think, feel, and act in relation to others. Interpretive scholars argue that people continually engage in the process of configuring and reconfiguring their experiences in order to make sense of them. From this vantage point, the constructions people create provide the basis for their interactions and help them navigate the personal and social labyrinths of everyday existence.

To say that human beings are involved in the social construction of reality is to suggest that the realm of experience cannot be understood in a completely neutral or objective manner. Interpretive scholars support the idea that lived experience is inherently subjective and is understood in a distinctly personal way. They acknowledge that the task of trying to gain insight into an individual's personal world is imperfect and not likely to be understood in its entirety, but they continue to pursue this goal, in spite of this uncertainty. In this sense, the difficulties involved in understanding the personal dimensions of human social life should not lead researchers to shy away from trying to learn more about them. On the contrary, the ambiguities of our existence are central to who we are and constitute the core of our personal and social lives—and are therefore essential to the domain of social research.

Interpretivists also argue that while these perceptions may differ from one individual to the next, they are not completely random, but are connected to the cultural practices, norms, and traditions of one's surroundings. From the standpoint of this orientation, there are clear ties between the worldviews of individuals and the shared frames of understanding they are exposed to through their interactions with family, peers, schoolmates, coworkers, and others they encounter in their everyday lives. While one's personal perspective may be unique, it is also formed and maintained in relation to the collective ways of seeing that are characteristic of that person's social environment.

This draws our attention to a key area of focus for interpretive social scientists, and that is culture. The concept of culture is vital to the work of interpretive scholars for a number of reasons, but the most significant of these is its connection to human consciousness. The expression "culture is to people as water is to a fish" is telling in that it illustrates both the pervasiveness and significance of culture while also revealing the lack of awareness many people have of it and its influence in their lives.

Defining culture in a traditional way may provide some insight into its meaning, but standard definitions often fail to do it justice. For instance, we could describe it as the values, norms, beliefs, practices, and traditions of a given group of people that are pervasive in their milieu. Or we could characterize it as "recorded culture" such as print, film, and other forms of media that connect individuals with others and help facilitate common modes of understanding among them. These would be technically accurate depictions of culture, but interpretivists would likely view them as only partial and missing the essence of what culture is about.

Culture from the point of view of this orientation is lived experience. It is the feeling we have of home, of our childhood, of family, and of friends. It is the sum of our experiences at school, including not only the cherished moments but the hard times and the bad memories we may have of the challenges we faced as individuals trying to belong while also wanting to assert our independence. For some, it may be living in survival mode from the moment of birth—facing poverty, war, or the constant fear of death. Culture is who we are. It is what we have become over the course of our lifetime, and it is a feeling of knowing the truth about ourselves and others—a feeling that we carry around in our hearts, as dear to us as life itself. We may be somewhat aware of it and reflect on it in a conscious way or we may simply be in it as a part of it, oblivious to its influence in our lives, but in either case, we are our culture as much as our culture is us.

The interpersonal and intimate nature of culture is one of the reasons people can have such a difficult time identifying it and stepping away from it to see it as an outsider. A typical pattern is for individuals to unconsciously embrace the values, beliefs, and traditions of their own cultural upbringing and internalize these so thoroughly that they seem to have originated from within themselves. Seeing culture this way helps clarify why some are so convinced they know the truth about the social world and that their interpretation of it is the only valid one. It also illustrates how it is possible for people raised in different cultures to have so much difficulty understanding one another and accepting ways of thinking and being that are contrary to their own. When we view culture as something living within us, we have a better sense of the kinds of conflict that can emerge from one group to the next, especially when questions of value and belief are at odds with one another.

From an interpretive point of view, the internalization of culture provides a foundation for the connections between social environment and individual consciousness. There is much more to our existence than consciousness, but this sphere constitutes such a central part of our existence that it gives us some clarity as to why it has become such an important focus of interpretive social scientists. Human beings do not simply create their own consciousness in isolation as though they were completely detached from their surroundings. They learn from experience and interaction with others about what they come to think of as right and wrong, good and bad, and what it means to find success or failure. Religious beliefs, secular values, and philosophical orientations are all developed in relation to the social world as individuals become who they are.

It is important to point out that interpretivists do not view socialization as something that simply happens to the individual, where a person is seen as a passive recipient of societal influences. They tend to take the position that while individuals are certainly connected to their social environments, they also actively decide how to decipher the goings on around them and turn these into meaningful experiences. Socialization is a powerful influence in this analysis, but it is inherently connected to the inclinations, affinities, thought processes, and choices of the individual along the way. People consciously participate in everyday connections with others and play an active role in shaping the directions and outcomes of their own lives and the lives of those with whom they interact.

This highlights an important distinguishing characteristic of the interpretive orientation, and that is while scholars in this tradition recognize the impact of social forces on individuals, they also place an emphasis on the role of agency as an interactive and influential component of social life. From this vantage point, the feelings, beliefs, and inner dialogues that constitute an individual's consciousness can lead to choices that differ significantly from the norm. People are indeed shaped by caregivers, peers, teachers, and media, but they also have the potential to think, feel, and act in ways that do not necessarily correspond to these social dynamics. From an interpretivist point of view, individuals have their own minds, their own hearts, and their own ability to deviate from the conventional practices and societal pressures surrounding them. Thought and action are neither the by-products of social structure nor the outcomes of absolute individuality. The social dimensions of everyday life have the potential to influence the individual, and the decisions people make have the potential to shape the direction of society and alter the course of history over time. Human agency is, in this sense, an integral factor in the formation and maintenance of the larger societal order.[50]

The assertion that there is a connection between culture, consciousness, and action also helps explain why interpretivists are inclined to object to the positivist pursuit of abstract laws and broader generalizations about the social world. From an interpretivist point of view, there is a significant degree of cultural variation from one region of the world to the next. As divergent social groups with qualitatively different ways of seeing the world interact with one another, there are culturally unique forms of consciousness and action that emerge in relation to these differences. Culture, consciousness, and the ways people choose to behave are context-specific and cannot be reduced to wholesale generalizations about the social world.

Their emphasis on the interactive nature of the relationship between culture, consciousness, and agency leads interpretive scholars to raise some challenging questions about social science. Are the dynamics underlying the perceptions of social scientists different from those of the people they study? Is it possible for social scientists to adopt a 'bird's eye' view of their subject matter or are they always embedded in a particular cultural framework? To what extent do social scientists rely on normative constructions as a way to make sense of the world around them and how might these be influencing their research?

Interpretive scholars argue that the subjective dimensions of human social life are unavoidable and have a clear impact on the work of social scientists. From within this orientation, all social issues are susceptible to the influences of embedded cultural norms and habits of thought. Whether one is referring to issues relating to class, race, gender, politics, mental health, or any other aspect of social life, the perspectives of researchers inevitably shape their inquiry. Their personal worldviews guide their work every step of the way, including their decisions about how to identify and select one research project over another, how to frame that research project, what concepts and categories to use to understand the topic, and what theories they draw on in developing their analyses and conclusions. The bottom line, from the standpoint of this orientation, is that there is no getting around the interpretive nature of social science.

Viewing social science in this way challenges traditional notions of what it means to be a researcher and how to think about the endeavor of social inquiry. Rather than conclude that one must make a choice between adopting the positivist orientation or giving up on the possibility of learning more about people in their social environments, interpretivists argue that insight into the subjective nature of social research can be harnessed as a way to break through the barriers put in place by positivism and create a pathway to developing more subtle and revealing ways of engaging in this endeavor.

An important step in working toward this goal is to address the need for reflexivity in the social sciences. Reflexivity in this context refers to the practice of social scientists taking into consideration the ways their own norms, traditions, and worldviews may be shaping their research. Accepting the idea that there are clear connections between social forces and individual perspectives means that social scientists must contemplate the possibility that this phenomenon is relevant to them as well. Recognizing this potential influence is the first step in acknowledging that social scientists are situated individuals, subject to the same kinds of dynamics occurring among the people they are studying. As individuals belonging to one cultural milieu or another, social scientists are embedded in the particular set of cultural norms, beliefs, and traditions they have internalized over time, and these invariably play a role in shaping how they understand and choose to act in the world. What interpretivism has shown us is that high-quality work is predicated on the willingness and ability of social scientists to acknowledge the presence of these influences in their own lives and think about them openly and critically.[51]

The challenges presented to social science by interpretivism are many. They involve coming to terms with the inexact nature of social research and contemplating the ways the worldviews of social scientists relate to their work. Meeting these challenges is no easy task because it means developing an awareness of something that scholars have unconsciously relied on for most of their lives and then reflecting on the ways this perspectival influence may be revised to enhance the purview of their research.

EVALUATING INTERPRETIVISM

This leads us to consider some of the principal strengths and weaknesses of interpretivism generally. Although interpretivism has managed to sidestep many of the problems associated with positivism and relativism, it does have its share of issues, and these are worth examining as a way to work toward a balanced epistemological orientation for the social sciences.

A key strength of interpretivism is its emphasis on the inherent differences that can be found when comparing the natural and social sciences. The inclination of social scientists to embrace the natural science paradigm has led some researchers to lose sight of the fundamentally human character of the people they are studying. This point is significant because it highlights the value in seeking to understand the more subjective and less tangible aspects of everyday life, such as religious conviction, human emotion, and the inner processes involved in the formation and maintenance of individual and collective consciousness. It can expose the centrality of these phenomena in people's lives and help researchers develop a view of cultural traditions in a range of social environments. Interpretivism stresses the importance in learning about what people believe and how they arrive at these beliefs over time. It encourages a focus on the ways feelings such as love, pride, sadness, anger, and joy can serve as powerful forces in producing and reproducing the world as it is today.

Another key contribution of this orientation to the social sciences is that it offers a mode of understanding the social world that does not fall into the trap of determinism. Its incorporation of agency and the actor's point of view provides a way for researchers to develop analyses of their subject matter that involves looking at the interplay between social forces and individual perceptions and their relationship to societal outcomes. Without this added dimension, social scientists have difficulty explaining situations where people fail to act as expected and choose instead to break with patterns of established behavior. Bringing agency into the equation helps them form analyses that are more comprehensive and better able to withstand critical scrutiny than those of the purely structural variety.

The interpretive orientation also enables researchers to examine social worlds that were previously hidden from view by bringing social science closer to the domain of interpersonal understanding. It is not possible to know exactly how people perceive themselves and the world around them, but there is certainly something to be said for working in this direction and striving to learn about ways the personal dimensions of social life relate to larger societal trends. Purveyors of this orientation have made significant strides toward this goal.

Having considered these strong points, we can move on to examine some of the shortcomings of interpretivism. One criticism facing this orientation is that its claim regarding the interpretive nature of social science interferes with the possibility of assessing the validity of competing analyses. Viewing social science as interpretive leaves one with some difficulty in gauging the relative merit of the many different ways to make sense of social phenomena. This opens the door to the proliferation of an endless array of conclusions and can undermine the potential of social science to collectively say anything of substance about past and present realities.[52]

From the standpoint of this critique, accepting the interpretive nature of social science limits the capacity of researchers to develop clear and consistent standards to determine what can be thought of as high-quality work. This lessens their ability to contribute to discussions about social issues as a collective entity. The questions arising in this regard are: What are the criteria interpretivists use when attempting to assess the caliber of social scientific analyses? How can scholars proclaiming the interpretive dimensions of social research determine the strength of their conclusions?[53]

These questions suggest that there is a basic need to develop a way to evaluate the quality of social research. While some interpretations of social phenomena may appear enlightening from one perspective, these same interpretations may seem misguided from another. How can scholars resolve these differences from within interpretivism? What is to prevent researchers from drawing on a particularly narrow-minded outlook as the basis for their research? The main grievance here is that the lack of a clear set of evaluative principles in interpretivism has the potential to disintegrate the field into an infinite number of perspectives, with little possibility for constructive conversation between competing factions. This fragmentation can undermine the legitimacy of social research on the whole and diminish its validity as a mode of inquiry and analysis.

A rebuttal to this argument is that the standards of interpretive research continue to remain high in spite of this diversity. Interpretive scholars are inclined to embrace the idea that high-caliber social inquiry requires a connection to empirical reality and a cogent theoretical framework. Accepting the possibility that a range of perspectives exists surrounding a given social issue does not imply that the integrity of the research is therefore compromised. Instead it means recognizing the fact that there can be many different ways of seeing social phenomena while maintaining an elevated level of rigor in every case.

In addition, the focus of interpretive researchers on reflexivity helps enhance the breadth of their work by enabling them to avoid the limitations of a culturally narrow viewpoint. They are, in this sense, bound by the standards and practices in their respective fields and expected to abide by these requirements even when operating interpretively. The fact that interpretivism allows for a range of perspectives can be seen as a strength when understood this way because it opens the door to ways of thinking about social phenomena that may not have been explored in the past. Rather than characterizing theoretical diversity as a crisis, interpretivists view it as a pathway to elevating the perspicacity of the social sciences on the whole.[54]

Another potential problem of interpretivism can be found in the tendency of researchers relying on this orientation to neglect the influence of larger societal forces on small-scale interaction. Critics argue that overlooking these macro-level forces can lead interpretive investigators to form analyses that miss the powerful environmental factors shaping micro-level phenomena.

Without taking these broader factors into consideration, interpretivist scholars are inclined to develop analyses that may appear insightful on the surface while actually leaving out important dimensions of the situation they are studying. From the standpoint of this critique, large-scale social forces penetrate into local environments and have a profound impact on the interactions of people situated within the confines of those environments.[55]

One example of this dynamic can be found in class stratification and the bearing it has on the opportunities and constraints facing individuals in different socioeconomic positions. Virtually all social scientists are familiar with the disparities in life chances that exist from one class stratum to the next, and most are aware of the impact of these divisions on the long-term trajectory of people's lives. Critics argue that a failure to take this kind of macro-level influence into account can lead researchers to miss the bigger picture and underestimate the ways political and economic factors relate to local culture and the consciousness of people situated in a given social environment. From this vantage point, it is problematic to focus exclusively on the subjective experiences of individuals and not examine the conditions they are required to deal with every day. Structural factors have a significant bearing on the lives of people in their social contexts and can alter their perspectives and the choices they make on a regular basis.

Critics of interpretivism also point out that the structural inequities associated with race and ethnicity have a clear connection to culture and consciousness as well. Studying race at the micro-level can certainly provide insight into the mindset of people and their interactions with others. This is obviously an important part of the equation, but critics argue that this closer examination may not adequately capture the ways institutional racism plays a part in shaping local situations and the micro-level processes unfolding in various contexts. From the point of view of this critique, the belief systems of people in a given culture are closely intertwined with the dominant institutional arrangements in that culture and these larger factors must be included when seeking to develop a comprehensive assessment of the situation being studied.

These are valid concerns, and interpretive scholars have addressed them in a variety of ways. One is to acknowledge the influence of social structure on small-scale interaction while also being mindful of the ways micro-level dynamics contribute to the formation and reformation of that structure. Rather than characterize social structure as a fixed entity determining social life, interpretive scholars are inclined to consider the ways interpersonal interactions taking place on a routine basis fit together to make up the social order. Interpretivists adopting this position argue that macro-level forces are certainly powerful but can also be seen as produced and reproduced on a regular basis through the interactions of individuals in their everyday lives.

Social forces are influential from this vantage point, but are created and maintained at the level of interpersonal interaction and are much more fluid than macro-level scholars are apt to acknowledge.[56]

This leads to a common misunderstanding of the interpretivist orientation generally, and that is the belief that it is only relevant to small-scale interaction and therefore solely applicable to micro-level research. An important response to this viewpoint is that the specific emphasis of interpretivism on feelings, beliefs, and personal perspectives places the focus of social inquiry on meaning and its relationship to human interaction. This is an orientation that need not be confined to small-scale research. There are clearly limitations in any effort to understanding people from outside their social milieu, but when scholars engaged in macro-level research weave this dimension of social life into their investigations, they can expand the breadth of their inquiry. Perception and emotion do not belong solely to the domain of micro-level research. These are integral components of all social phenomena and are essential elements in any social scientific investigation.

The call to better understand phenomena related to consciousness, meaning, and emotion does present an epistemological challenge to the social scientist, but interpretive researchers persist in their efforts to learn about this domain and have achieved some success in doing so. Although it certainly possesses some limitations, the interpretive orientation provides us with a viable alternative to positivism and relativism in its demonstration that it is possible to study the subjective dimensions of everyday life in a scientific manner. It suggests ways to contend with the less tangible dimensions of social phenomena and offers significant insight into the interplay between agency and structure. As social scientists gain an awareness of the connections between their own perspectives and the substance of their investigations, they are better able to address these issues and improve the quality of their work. Being cognizant of these connections is the first step in the journey to engaging in high-level research. Making an effort to avoid objectifying or oversimplifying the individuals, groups, and large-scale social processes they are studying can take interpretive researchers some distance toward developing innovative and revealing analyses and conclusions.

Rather than seeing the task of social research as the attempt to capture a photograph-like image of one's subject matter and sharing that image with others, one might think of it as producing a painting that sheds new light on a particular dimension of the social world that is not readily apparent to the casual observer. Taking this approach can help others understand it in ways they may not have considered before. We can thus depict the work of interpretive researchers as being concerned with the goal of drawing attention to social phenomena that would otherwise remain obscured or poorly understood without the benefit of this orientation and its associated forms of investigation.

In sum, interpretivism offers a substantial contribution to the development of a balanced epistemological orientation for the social sciences. It opens the door to hidden social worlds and takes us closer to understanding the imprecise realm of human consciousness. While it may not be possible to know exactly how others perceive the world or why they do what they do, there is certainly some value in striving to work in this direction. The interpretive emphases on meaning and the personal dimensions of everyday life are central to the ongoing effort to understand the connections between individual experience and broader societal trends. The interpretive orientation is certainly not infallible, but it has done a formidable job in clarifying the ideas and practices needed to reach this goal.

NOTES

1. For a concise portrayal of some of the central ideas of hermeneutics, please see: Jens Zimmerman, *Hermeneutics: A Very Short Introduction* (Oxford: Oxford University Press, 2015).

2. Wilhelm Dilthey, *Descriptive Psychology and Historical Understanding*, trans. Richard M. Zaner and Kenneth L. Heiges (The Hague: Martinus Nuhoff, 1977; orig. pub. 1924), 123–44.

3. Dilthey, *Descriptive Psychology*, 123–44.

4. Wilhelm Dilthey, *The Formation of the Historical World in the Human Sciences: Selected Works of Wilhem Dilthey, Volume III* (Princeton, NJ: Princeton University Press, 2002; orig. pub. 1910), 101–212.

5. Dilthey, *The Formation of the Historical World*, 132–35.

6. For more on this please see: Hans-Georg Gadamer, "Boundaries of Language," in *Language and Linguisticality in Gadamer's Hermeneutics* (New York, NY: Lexington Books, 2000), 9–17.

7. This issue is addressed more fully in: Paul Ricoeur, *Hermeneutics and the Human Sciences: Essays on Language, Action, and Interpretation*, trans. and ed. John B. Thompson (Cambridge: Cambridge University Press, 1981).

8. For more on this issue, please see: Karl-Otto Apel, "Regulative Ideas or Sense-Events? An Attempt to Determine the Logos of Hermeneutics," in *The Question of Hermeneutics: Essays in Honor of Joseph J. Kockelmans*, ed. Timothy J. Stapleton (New York, NY: Springer, 1994).

9. Ricoeur, *Hermeneutics and the Human Sciences*.

10. Michael Polanyi and Harry Prosch, *Meaning* (Chicago, IL: University of Chicago Press, 1996).

11. Ricoeur, *Hermeneutics and the Human Sciences*.

12. An insightful portrayal of this position can be found in: Richard Bernstein, "From Hermeneutics to Praxis," *Review of Metaphysics* 35, no. 4 (1982): 823–45.

13. Bernstein, "From Hermeneutics to Praxis," 823–45.

14. Bernstein, "From Hermeneutics to Praxis," 823–45.

15. Please see: Hans-Georg Gadamer, *Truth and Method* (New York, NY: Continuum, 1997).

16. Gadamer, *Truth and Method*, 302–5.

17. For a brief overview of Weber's life and work, please see the introduction to: *From Max Weber: Essays in Sociology*, trans. Hans Gerth and C. Wright Mills (New York, NY: Oxford University Press, 1958), 3–74.

18. Weber outlines this position most clearly in: "Bureaucracy," in *From Max Weber*, 196–244.

19. Please see: Weber, *From Max Weber*, 228–44.

20. Weber presents this view in: "Science as a Vocation," *From Max Weber*, 129–56.

21. Weber, "Science as a Vocation," *From Max Weber*, 129–56.

22. Please see: Max Weber, *The Methodology of the Social Sciences*, trans. and ed. Edward Shils and Henry Finch (New York, NY: The Free Press, 1949; orig. pub. 1903–1917).

23. Max Weber, *The Protestant Ethic and the Spirit of Capitalism*, trans. Talcott Parsons (New York, NY: Charles Scribner's Sons, 1958; orig. pub. 1904).

24. Max Weber, *The Theory of Social and Economic Organization*, trans. A. M. Henderson and Talcott Parsons (New York, NY: Oxford University Press, 1947).

25. For more on this, please see, Weber, *The Methodology of the Social Sciences*.

26. Weber, "Science as a Vocation," and "Politics as a Vocation," *From Max Weber*, 77–156.

27. Weber, "Science as a Vocation," and "Politics as a Vocation," *From Max Weber*, 77–156.

28. Weber, "Science as a Vocation," *From Max Weber*, 129–56. Also, for more on Weber's epistemological orientation and his contribution to the interpretive orientation, please see: Charles Gattone, "Max Weber: Social Science and Politics in the Transition to State Capitalism," in *The Social Scientist as Public Intellectual: Critical Reflections in a Changing World* (Lanham, MD: Rowman & Littlefield, 2006), 21–34.

29. Edmund Husserl, *The Crisis of European Sciences and Transcendental Phenomenology: An Introduction to Phenomenological Philosophy* (Evanston, IL: Northwestern University Press, 1954, 1970; orig. pub. 1936).

30. Edmund Husserl, *Ideas Pertaining to a Pure Phenomenology and to a Phenomenological Philosophy – First Book: General Introduction to a Pure Phenomenology*, trans. F. Kersten (The Hague: Nijhoff, 1982; orig. pub. 1913), 1005–130.

31. Husserl discusses this idea in: Edmund Husserl, *Logical Investigations, Volume 2* (Milton Park: Routledge, 2006; orig. pub. 1901) and in *Ideas – First Book*, Sections 90–94, pp. 217–31.

32. Edmund Husserl, *Cartesian Meditations*, trans. J. S. Churchill and K. Ameriks (London: Routledge, 1973; orig. pub. 1931).

33. This is a translation of Husserl, from: "Elements of a Science of the Lifeworld," in *The Essential Husserl: Basic Writings in Transcendental Phenomenology* (Bloomington, IN: Indiana University Press, 1999), 367. It was originally extracted from Husserl's unfinished work: *The Crisis of European Sciences and Transcendental Phenomenology*.

34. Husserl discusses the concept of the natural attitude in *Ideas – First Book*, 56–238.

35. Husserl, *Ideas – First Book*, 147–238.

36. Husserl, *Ideas – First Book*, 37–156.

37. Husserl, *Ideas – First Book*, 61–69.

38. Husserl, *Ideas – First Book*, 61–238.

39. Husserl, *Ideas – First Book*, 37–238.

40. Husserl wrote about the consciousness of internal time in: Husserl, *Ideas – First Book*, Sec. 114, pp. 268–78. Schütz was influenced by Henri Bergson on this matter. He discussed the concept of the stream of experience in: Alfred Schütz, *The Phenomenology of the Social World* (Evanston, IL: Northwestern University Press, 1967), 45–53.

41. Schütz, *The Phenomenology*, 45–53.

42. Schütz, *The Phenomenology*, 12–20.

43. Schütz, *The Phenomenology*, 12–20.

44. Alfred Schütz, "The Social World and the Theory of Social Action," *Social Research* 27, no. 2 (Summer, 1960): 203–21.

45. Schütz, "The Social World."

46. For additional insight into Schütz's position on this matter, please see: Alfred Schütz, "Common-Sense and Scientific Interpretation of Human Action," *Philosophy and Phenomenological Research* XIV, no. 1 (September 1953).

47. This quote is from: Schütz, "The Social World," 206.

48. Schütz presented this view in: Schütz, "Common-Sense and Scientific Interpretation," 1–38.

49. Schütz, "Common-Sense and Scientific Interpretation," 1–38.

50. Herbert Blumer outlined this view most clearly in: Herbert Blumer, *Symbolic Interactionism* (Englewood Cliffs, NJ: Prentice-Hall, 1969).

51. Pierre Bourdieu discussed the concept of reflexivity in: Pierre Bourdieu, "Vive la Crise! For Heterodoxy in Social Science," *Theory and Society* 17, no. 5 (1988): 773–87.

52. Schütz raises these issues in: "Some Basic Problems of Interpretive Sociology," in *The Phenomenology of the Social World*, 215–24.

53. Schütz, *The Phenomenology*, 215–24.

54. Bourdieu presents this view in: "Vive la Crise!," 773–87.

55. For more on this topic, please see: Michael Williams, *Problems of Knowledge: A Critical Introduction to Epistemology* (Oxford: Oxford University Press, 2001).

56. W. E. B. DuBois approached the topic of race from the point of view of both the institutional and interpersonal factors involved. When discussing the concept of race, he generally referred to it as "the race idea," drawing attention to the socially constructed nature of this concept. Please see: W. E. B. DuBois, *The Social Theory of W.E.B. DuBois* (New York, NY: Sage, 2004). For another example of this way of thinking, please see: Sheldon Stryker, *Symbolic Interactionism* (Caldwell, NJ: Blackburn Press, 2003).

Chapter 4

Intersubjectivism

The Quest for Common Ground

Having taken a look at some of the strengths and weaknesses of positivism, relativism, and interpretivism, we can now move on to examine intersubjectivism and its connections to the social sciences. The term "intersubjective" refers to a mode of thought that is not limited to individual or "subjective" points of view but includes a variety of perspectives integrated together as a unified whole. Purveyors of the intersubjective orientation accept the idea that there are significant differences in the ways people interpret their surroundings, but they also argue that some degree of overlap exists even among those whose differences appear to be irreconcilable—and it is through these connections that people are able to communicate and interact with one another. From an intersubjectivist point of view, ties of this nature can serve as a means to establishing common ground in the realm of ideas and in the activities of the everyday world.

Our investigation into this epistemological orientation begins with a review of some of the social thinkers whose work provided its starting foundation. These range from scholars in the area of phenomenology to those associated with pragmatism and critical theory. Intersubjectivism brings together elements from a variety of perspectives and synthesizes them into a relatively consistent and comprehensive set of conclusions about the nature of knowledge and truth. These ideas have not only broadened the debate regarding the philosophy of social science, but they have enhanced discussions of politics and culture outside academia as well.

PHENOMENOLOGY

In chapter 3 of this book, we observed the role phenomenology played in the development of interpretivism, but it is important to point out that authors writing in this tradition also contributed to the formation of intersubjectivism. Edmund Husserl, Alfred Schütz, and others in this camp helped forge the conceptual framework of the intersubjective orientation by highlighting the interpersonal dimensions of consciousness and the collective nature of understanding. These social thinkers focused on the connections people have with one another in their daily lives, and they outlined the significance of communication in the domain of social science and in society broadly.

Continuing our discussion of Husserl from chapter 3, we can reiterate his claim that perception is at the core of everyday life, where people make sense of the world in accordance with the ways they interpret their experiences. Husserl also expressed the position that consciousness is something that develops in relation to the interactions one has with others, where elements of culture such as norms, traditions, and beliefs are closely tied to one's sense of truth. In Husserl's analysis, although the lifeworld is experienced as being personal and private, the human craving for interaction gives it a social dimension and renders it an inherently intersubjective phenomenon. Individual consciousness is indeed unique to each person, but it is also connected to the collective consciousness of one's surrounding milieu and not entirely independent of external influences. Personal perception and inclination intersect with social experience, and this, in turn, has a significant bearing on the worldview and sense of truth one develops internally.[1]

ALFRED SCHÜTZ

Schütz added to this analysis by claiming that individuals develop their own identity in large part through communication and interaction with others. He went as far as to suggest that human consciousness develops in such a way as to give primacy to what he called the "we" over the "I." By this he meant that as children are socialized to form a sense of their surrounding milieu, they initially see the group of which they are a part—family, friends, and community—as the entirety of their existence. It is only after establishing this notion of the collective that they begin to develop an awareness of themselves as independent individuals existing apart from others. Schütz's claim in this regard is that our understanding of who we are is predicated on our conception of those around us and our sense of how they perceive us.[2]

Both Husserl and Schütz pointed out that language provides a key element of the framework of understanding people rely on in their everyday lives. The words we use on a regular basis have an embedded set of shared meanings that enable us to understand and communicate with one another. These shared meanings provide us with a way to make sense of what others are saying and doing and respond in a manner that can be understood by them as well. From this point of view, the conceptual frames embedded in words serve as the basis for mutual understanding in a variety of social contexts.[3]

This point is fundamental to the intersubjective orientation because it illustrates the significance of social interaction in the formation of individual consciousness and in the construction of one's sense of self. Husserl and Schütz suggested that any attempt to understand the individual must take into consideration the connections between the personal and the social. Human beings do have the potential for independent thought, but they are also part of a larger societal order where the ideas, beliefs, and practices they adopt over time are connected to others. In phenomenology, the interpersonal dimensions of everyday life are at the core of individual worldview and serve as an important element in the formation of who we are and how we think.[4]

PRAGMATISM

Focusing on the interpersonal nature of consciousness illustrates the social dimensions of individual perception and leads us to a discussion of pragmatism and its unique contribution to the intersubjective orientation. The early pragmatist scholars forged an alternative to the prevailing modes of thought in the United States and Europe in the early 1900s, challenging some of the conventional trends in philosophy and creating new ways to conceptualize and study the social world. Charles Peirce, William James, and John Dewey are among the principal authors who helped build the foundation for this somewhat atypical philosophical tradition. Their work in this area has been influential in reorienting the foundations of Western social thought and in shifting the intellectual debate on the nature of truth. Taking a brief look at their ideas will provide us with some insight into the specifics of pragmatism and inform our discussion regarding intersubjectivism and its significance as an epistemological orientation for the social sciences.

CHARLES PEIRCE

Charles Sanders Peirce was one of the initial social thinkers to develop the foundational ideas of pragmatist thought. Peirce was a philosopher, mathematician, logician, and expert in the area of semiotics. His focus on epistemology stemmed from his concern to address some of the problems associated with consciousness and communication as they relate to the formation of new knowledge. His multifaceted background and wide range of expertise enabled him to provide a unique contribution to epistemology and the philosophy of social science.[5]

Peirce developed his ideas from within the framework of formal logic, and while he supported many of the premises of this mode of thought, he also observed some of its salient limitations. He maintained that while logic provided a valuable way to clarify thinking on a number of social issues, it could not of its own accord address the practical questions of everyday life. From Peirce's point of view, for any theoretical conceptualization to be meaningful, it must have a link to empirical reality as experienced by those living in it. Ideas existing solely in the abstract can offer only a partial understanding of practical reality and are typically less enlightening than those holding a direct connection to the real world. With this in mind, Peirce sought to construct an epistemological orientation that moved from the realm of abstract speculation to that of practical experience.[6]

To do this, he proposed reconceptualizing some of the central ideas of conventional European philosophy and developing a mode of thought for social inquiry that addresses these observations. Peirce noted that mainstream philosophy did offer some insight into the ways people make sense of their surroundings. He pointed to the example of Descartes and Leibniz and their positions regarding the strategies people use to develop new knowledge. Drawing on the work of these philosophers, Peirce highlighted two grades of clarity that provide the means through which to understand the concepts used in the development of knowledge. The first of these is that which one can attain through an experiential encounter with a concept. For instance, holding one's hand near a flame enables a person to develop an experiential sense of heat. This understanding of heat, while instructive, is rather rudimentary since it is based solely on immediate experience and does not tell us much beyond this initial personal encounter. The second grade of clarity offered by Descartes and Leibniz involves thinking of a concept in the abstract and being able to formulate a working definition of it in theoretical terms. In the example of heat, we can define it as energy that exists when the atoms and molecules of a particular substance vibrate more rapidly than when they are cooler, resulting in that substance having a higher temperature. Thinking of heat in the abstract thus provides us with a more elaborate understanding of the concept than that which we can ascertain when relying on experience alone.[7]

Peirce argued that while this two-dimensional way of knowing can lead to an initial understanding of a concept, it is still limited in the sense that it presents a rather static version of it—as if it were fixed and set apart from all other concepts. To add to this initial schema, he proposed a third grade of clarity, and this involves considering the practical dimensions of concepts to understand them more completely. The main principle of this third grade of clarity is that in order to more fully comprehend a particular concept, researchers need to develop a sense of the consequences that can be expected to occur if their understanding of that concept is valid. That is to say that an understanding of a phenomenon can be enhanced if investigators reflect on the ways it interacts with other aspects of the world on a routine basis.[8]

So, in our examination of heat, we may notice that when paper is near a flame, it begins to burn. We thus surmise that when other objects are near a flame, they may begin to burn as well. Testing this hypothesis and learning about the consequences of real-life interaction tell us a great deal more about heat than we could know from our immediate experience or from an abstract definition alone.[9]

> In order to ascertain the meaning of an intellectual conception one should consider what practical consequences might result by necessity from the truth of that conception; and the sum of these consequences will constitute the entire meaning of the conception.[10]

Peirce argued that thinking of phenomena in this manner can help strengthen our understanding of them. He called this "the pragmatic maxim," stating that this third grade of clarity enables us to move beyond the limitations of conventional techniques of gaining knowledge and toward new insight into the interactive dimensions of everyday life.[11]

WILLIAM JAMES

William James expanded Peirce's ideas on this topic by weaving them into a broader theoretical framework about the nature of truth. James argued that a concept only has meaning for people when it connects to their current reality and demonstrates some relevance to their existing understanding of the world. He disagreed with the Hegelian notion that a heightened sense of truth can emerge through the use of logic or dialectical reasoning alone and contended that, in everyday life, people draw on their own experiences and perceptions to determine the truthfulness of a particular idea. Claims about the social world are thus perceived as true when they resonate with one's sense of the facts and the ways those facts are assumed to be connected to one another. His conception of truth is one that takes into account the role of existing beliefs as well as the material and practical conditions involved in the formation of knowledge.[12]

James did not see truth about social phenomena as absolute or fixed, but as something that can change over time as new evidence and new ways of making sense of the world emerge. Truth, from James' point of view is connected to practical reality and should be thought of as provisional rather than universal in nature. What is perceived to be true in one context may be seen as false in another, and this discrepancy does not diminish the validity of either assertion in its current form. Conceiving of truth as provisional does not mean ignoring the facts or denying the existence of empirical evidence. It means focusing one's attention on the ways facts are formed and how they are brought together in conjunction with common modes of thinking in order to understand them in a coherent manner.[13]

This view of truth led James to reject the notion of determinism—the belief that the fate of one's life, community, or society as a whole could somehow be determined by structural factors, where the choices and actions of individuals have little or no bearing on the course of history. He saw determinism as connected to the belief that the social order operates as a mechanism subject to universal laws and inevitable trends. According to James, people may, at times, make choices in a calculating fashion, but they have also been known to act on the basis of emotion and whim and in ways that do not necessarily conform to preexisting expectations. When dealing with human beings, there are often unforeseen factors that come into play, and this means that their thoughts, feelings, and actions cannot be predicted in a formulaic manner.[14]

James supported this claim by considering the possibility of free will. He argued that while social forces are certainly powerful in shaping people's consciousness, they do not determine it. In James' analysis, free will exists even in situations where it appears as though structural factors dominate the lives of everyone living within a particular social system.

> I think that yesterday was a crisis in my life. I finished the first part of Renouvier's second Essais and see no reason why his definition of free will—"the sustaining of a thought because I choose to when I might have other thoughts"—need be the definition of an illusion. At any rate, I will assume for the present—until next year—that it is no illusion. My first act of free will shall be to believe in free will.[15]

From James' point of view, one can choose to believe in an idea even though there may be insufficient evidence to support it in the present moment. He argued that this premise is in many ways at odds with the tenets of mainstream science, but he maintained that it is absolutely necessary as a prerequisite to living everyday life. In order to navigate the challenges of our own existence, we must rely on at least a minimal level of unsubstantiated assumptions. In the absence of this practice, we would be severely hindered in our ability to engage in even the simplest of tasks, including interacting with others. James understood that the tension between social forces and free will varies significantly from one context to the next, but he argued that there are times when societal pressures may seem to have a heavier influence over the lives of individuals than they actually do, and it is in these moments that the decision of the individual to either believe in or doubt free will can have significant consequences.[16]

While he argued in favor of the presence of free will and individual freedom of thought, James did not accept the claim of subjectivism that truth can only be understood in terms of the unique worldview of each individual. He contended that ideas have a social dimension to them and are formed in relation to shared norms and values. He did not portray the social world as a collection of individuals where everyone has the freedom to act entirely on the basis of their own immediate impulses, but saw people as being connected through common assumptions about themselves and the world around them. He took the position that there is an interplay between the consciousness of individuals and the expectations people have regarding the consequences of any behavior. It is the interaction of these intangibles that forms the basis of social life and ultimately has a bearing on the course of human history.[17]

James concluded that the interactive dynamics of the social world are less calculable than the proponents of universals claim. From his perspective, people can be better understood when viewed in terms of their innately human character. In order to comprehend the subtleties of social life, one must try to learn more about the meanings individuals attribute to their experience and the ways contextual factors and interpersonal beliefs relate to the kinds of decisions they make every day. The ideas and actions of human beings do indeed follow patterns at times, but these patterns do not reflect the physics of inanimate objects. Rather than characterizing thought and action as mere functions of the structural constraints and cultural expectations in a given society, James argued that the ever-present dance between individuals and the social world can manifest itself in unexpected ways and yield unanticipated results. The effort to understand people thus requires one to consider the intersubjective dimensions of everyday life and the ongoing interactions involved in the formation of new knowledge.[18]

JOHN DEWEY

John Dewey further developed the ideas of Peirce and James to contribute to pragmatism with a concern to help build and maintain viable participatory democracies in the United States and throughout the Western world. His assessment of American society focused on the growing factions within the populace that divided the country, fostering misunderstanding and dissension and interfering with the nation's ability to move forward in an enlightened and democratic fashion. He observed the ways public discussions of political issues tended to drift toward polar extremes, leading members of various sectors of the population to be swayed by unsubstantiated claims and emotional appeals. Dewey sought to address the problems associated with finding truth at a time when an emphasis on reason and logic seemed to be slipping away. He hoped to challenge these trends and work toward the development of a more stable and well-grounded basis for social thought that could serve as a guide for culture and politics in the modern world.[19]

Dewey contended that, in a democratic society, political conflict cannot be adequately resolved in a laissez-faire manner. From his point of view, even though there may be different groups with varied interests and competing perspectives, public policy requires some degree of consensus about which steps to take collectively. A central condition of politics is the need to bring together opposing parties to hash out their differences and establish at least a minimal level of agreement in order to be able to engage in cooperative action. In making these kinds of decisions, there is an inescapable requirement that people communicate with one another and find common ground— with the goal of moving in a relatively unified direction. Pragmatism, in Dewey's analysis, involves developing an informed populace that is willing and able to work cooperatively to cultivate intelligent and insightful decisions in matters of public affairs. Without this starting foundation, the risk of authoritarianism grows and the possibility of maintaining a viable democracy shrinks to the point of disappearing altogether.[20]

Dewey thus expanded the ideas of Peirce and James by arguing that there is a crucial need in modern democracies to adopt a pragmatic understanding of the social world as a way to bring reasoned knowledge into the domain of politics. He criticized the mainstream tenets of social science that drew on the positivist notion of searching for truth in a manner that emulated the natural sciences. Instead, he emphasized the point that constructing knowledge about the social world is an interactive and collective endeavor. In Dewey's analysis, social inquiry cannot escape the influence of perspective in shaping the practices that are commonplace in one's field. Social scientific truths exist in relation to the cultural frameworks investigators create to carry out their research projects, and these truths are closely connected to the practical circumstances involved in their production.[21]

Dewey's emphasis on the pragmatic character of knowledge did not lead him to embrace a relativist conception of truth. He rejected the idea that the only alternative to the positivist orientation was the subjectivist approach to understanding knowledge. Instead, he focused on the unavoidable requirement that knowledge be connected to an initial starting point in order for it to develop and grow into a viable analysis with some degree of relevance to politics and the social world broadly. His goal was to find a practical way to build that foundation—one that brought together conflicting perspectives, empirical evidence, and a reliance on reasoned discussion as a way to forge common ground. Without a minimal level of consensus, knowledge becomes fragmented and the potential for democracy diminishes, threatening the opportunity for self-determination and individual freedom.[22]

This leads us to a discussion of the connections Dewey observed between knowledge and ethics. His position on this matter is that ways of knowing about the social world are connected to value judgments and a collective sense of right and wrong. In Dewey's analysis, each form of knowledge not only comprises an underlying set of beliefs about reality but also embodies implicit claims about the ideas and actions that are thought to be virtuous and just. He argued that the effort to search for a universal set of ethics is inherently flawed because it fails to acknowledge the normative nature of consciousness and value judgments in the everyday world. Decisions about what constitutes an ethical way to interact with others can vary significantly from one cultural context to another. Deeply held values in a particular society may be perceived as misguided when seen from an alternative viewpoint. Dewey's primary assertion in this regard is that, while the conceptual framework of a given group shapes their notion of truth, it also shapes what is seen from their perspective as ethical.[23]

Dewey's emphasis on this connection and his concerns regarding the need for mutual understanding led him to advocate an approach to the formation of knowledge that focused on social interaction and collective deliberation. The culturally normative nature of truth and the role of worldview in the constitution of knowledge and ethics render the essence of these domains uncertain. They are therefore prone to the whims of public opinion and demagogic leadership and may be arbitrarily influenced by corrupt and deceptive political groups. His response to this concern was to argue that the formation of new knowledge should be guided by informed empirical observation, debate and discussion, reasoned analysis, and a mindful consideration of the consequences involved. He advocated a path to truth that employs the insights of traditional philosophy, pragmatism, and critical thinking as a guide to developing an informed and enlightened set of directions over time.[24]

From this brief overview, we can begin to cultivate some insight into the basic ideas of pragmatism and its connections to the intersubjective orientation. This introduction shows us that pragmatism focuses on the problem of ambiguity in knowledge and ethics as they relate to social phenomena. This philosophy is centered on the challenges involved in the search for meaning and in the effort to construct ways of knowing that can yield new and relevant modes of understanding. Pragmatists contend that without this starting point, neither knowledge nor ethics can be created or maintained in a coherent manner. Their position is that some grounding is needed as a prerequisite to forming viable ways of making sense of the everyday world and acting in it.

Pragmatists argue that when groups of people come together and work toward consensus on a range of issues, their conclusions can serve as the basis for developing new knowledge and forming a collective sense of direction. They view this consensus as legitimate, but do not see it as universally objective or as being beyond the realm of interpretation. The epistemological grounding created through consensus is, in this sense, provisional. It is something that may be transformed in the future as new evidence and ideas emerge. Although it is not absolute, it can nevertheless provide the footing for socially relevant and empirically verifiable ways of knowing.[25]

In addition to challenging the positivist notion that the social world exists as a transcendent reality, pragmatists reject the relativist contention that reality is solely a matter of individual perspective. Their emphasis on the idea of constructing knowledge through informed debate and discussion is an indication of their effort to move beyond the limitations of these orientations and carve out a viable path for the philosophy of social science. Scholars writing in this tradition seek to bring the quest for new knowledge closer to the domain of practical reality by connecting it to experience and the human dimensions of everyday life.

CRITICAL THEORY

Focusing on the connections between collective experience and truth leads us to a discussion of critical theory and its contributions to intersubjectivism. It is important to preface this section with the point that the early critical theorists were not themselves advocates of an epistemological orientation that could be characterized as uniquely intersubjective. Their approach tended to be somewhat eclectic and intuitive in nature and relied on a broad range of theoretical perspectives. The views of these authors are nevertheless integral to our discussion in that they constituted a springboard for the work of later critical theorists and for the intersubjective orientation on the whole.[26]

The early critical theorists developed their ideas about modern society in the midst of the Nazi rise to power in Germany in the 1930s. Max Horkheimer, Theodor Adorno, Herbert Marcuse, Walter Benjamin, and others witnessed firsthand the ways the Nazi regime used carefully studied and highly rationalized methods of societal management to achieve their goal of consolidating power. According to these authors, the strategies of the Nazis served as an example of the ways mechanizing the organization of the social order can lead to a brutally effective form of institutional domination and authoritarian control.[27]

They observed this pattern occurring in other parts of the world as well, including the former Soviet Union, where political repression evolved in conjunction with the centralization of power. They characterized this phenomenon as part of a larger transformation threatening to undermine the potential for individual freedom on a global scale. In their eyes, this trend grew out of aspects of modernity that were unforeseen by the early Enlightenment thinkers and ironically moved society in a regressive direction. Rather than viewing rationality as contributing to an increasingly advanced state over time, they expressed concern that it was leading humanity down the path of civilizational decline.[28]

This generation of critical theorists observed that one of the key strategies used by authoritarian regimes to achieve and maintain power involved the deliberate manipulation of knowledge and public opinion. They took note of the fact that political officials in these regimes developed sophisticated techniques of framing knowledge to infuse their own "truths" into the public sphere. The primary argument of critical theory in this regard is that the practice of systematically refining the strategies of knowledge production over time and employing these strategies broadly helped burgeoning dictatorships around the world gain popular support and guide society toward totalitarian objectives. Institutional leaders routinely disseminated misinformation throughout society as a way to steer political discourse in their preferred direction and maintain a strong grip on collective consciousness. The success of authoritarianism was, in this sense, closely linked to the systematic manipulation of knowledge and management of public opinion on a grand scale.[29]

In addition to this phenomenon, Horkheimer and Adorno observed a trend unfolding in capitalist societies generally, where the rise of popular culture and entertainment in media proved to be enticing and capable of leading members of the general population to become more passive and accepting of the dominant worldview. This attitude of acquiescence magnified their susceptibility to institutionally derived frames of knowledge and further enhanced the power of political and economic organizations. Horkheimer and Adorno characterized this as "the culture industry," arguing that the institutional production of knowledge, values, and beliefs had the effect of shaping public opinion and leading throngs of people to become naive supporters of establishmentarian modes of understanding.[30]

The early critical theorists presented the overriding argument that the never-ending supply of official propaganda and popular culture together contribute to values and ways of thinking that help government and business organizations achieve their goals. As members of the general population come to adopt media-based frames of understanding, they are increasingly inclined to support autocratic policies that diminish individual freedom. A result of this phenomenon is that original ideas created by people at the interpersonal level decline while institutional perspectives grow in popularity to become a permanent fixture in the domain of everyday life. Knowledge in this context is a tool of the authorities, employed in the service of administrative management and maintained as a way to guide individual and collective consciousness toward the widespread acceptance of officially sanctioned ideals.[31]

The early critical theorists thus formed an extremely pessimistic view of the directions of modern society, where centralized authority led to the ideological domination and institutional control of large swaths of the population. Although these thinkers favored a fair and balanced form of public discourse, they were not hopeful that this level of independence could be achieved in a modern context. Their resulting conclusions regarding the nature of knowledge centered on the structural constraints obscuring the potential for freedom of thought and action and highlighted the ways dominant institutions had taken the helm in the formation of new ideas.[32]

JÜRGEN HABERMAS

While the early critical theorists were not optimistic in their assessment of modern society, subsequent authors writing in this tradition did see some hope for individual freedom in the future. One of the more prominent philosophers taking this view was Jürgen Habermas. Habermas drew on the ideas of critical theory, but he also integrated the work of social thinkers outside this school of thought into his analysis. His contribution to intersubjectivism can be seen as broadly influenced by several philosophies in addition to critical theory, including pragmatism, phenomenology, Marxism, and hermeneutics. This diverse background endowed the intersubjective orientation with a uniquely expansive theoretical focus while also synthesizing disparate ideas into a fairly unified and comprehensive form.[33]

Habermas conceded that modern society was not unfolding as the early Enlightenment thinkers had hoped, but he saw room for positive social change. He drew on the notion of the lifeworld employed by the phenomenologists in constructing his theoretical framework, but coming out of the tradition of critical theory, he also considered the ways larger structural factors such as those associated with politics and economy relate to personal experience and perception. Habermas argued that in modern society, the requirements of the system gradually weave their way into people's personal lives, shaping the ideas, beliefs, and practices that become accepted as commonplace in the lifeworld. In his analysis, the rationalized nature of the system pushes the lifeworld toward mechanized and impersonal forms of thought and action. He suggested that this leads people toward an enhanced devotion to the system and inhibits their potential to think independently. The goals of the system—for example, efficiency, effectiveness, and a dedicated adherence to institutional directives—come to dominate the lifeworld, filtering into people's everyday consciousness and shaping their ways of seeing themselves and others.[34]

Habermas depicted this trend as being connected to the diminishing quality of public discourse in contemporary society. He observed that the level of discussion and debate regarding social, political, and economic issues exhibited a steady decline over the course of modern history, and he expressed concern regarding the consequences of this in terms of human emancipation and self-determination. In his analysis, mass media, popular culture, and the expanded use of obscurantist political rhetoric tend to push public discourse in the direction of oversimplified and one-sided perspectives. This undermines the potential for informed democratic participation and contributes to increasingly centralized and authoritarian forms of government.[35]

In spite of these concerns, however, Habermas expressed hope regarding the potential for independent thinking and enlightened discussion in the public sphere. He suggested that an alternative to the trend toward institutional domination could be found in the domain of communication. From his vantage point, although the organizational dynamics of the system can diminish the quality of public discourse, the lifeworld has the ability to push back against this trend through communicative action. To support this position, he drew on Dewey's contention that building a viable democracy requires open debate where all participants have a voice in shaping the ideas that eventually come to prevail throughout society. Habermas suggested that attaining this goal is possible due to the inherently social nature of human beings and their innate drive to communicate with one another. The fact that people have a fundamental need to interact with each other opens the door to the possibility of sharing ideas and values in an uninhibited manner—in what he called an "ideal speech situation." The primary goal of this approach, in Habermas' view, is to rely on the drive for interaction as a way to facilitate open communication among individuals and groups rather than continuing to draw on institutional frames as a guide for the development of new ideas and new knowledge.[36]

Habermas recognized the difficulties involved in attaining an ideal speech situation and described this as something to work toward rather than an end point that can exist in pure form. In his view, knowledge constructed through open communication has the potential to serve as a countervailing force to the encroachment of the system on the lifeworld. Open communication allows for the development of perspectives that originate at an interpersonal level instead of in the domain of institutional authority. He argued that the creation of new knowledge is not necessarily at the mercy of institutional ideals and objectives but can be established collectively and in ways that provide at least some independence from the pressures of the system.[37]

This analysis is relevant to the social sciences in that it draws attention to the uphill battle researchers face in their efforts to develop knowledge that is independent of institutional influence. Habermas contended that academic institutions are part of the system and, as such, are inclined to serve its interests, but he also maintained that communicative action can enable scholars to push back against these pressures and act in an autonomous and self-directed manner. When social scientists recognize the need to think independently and refrain from uncritically embracing institutional expectations and directives, they can elevate the quality of their research and develop original and innovative analyses. In Habermas' view, there is room for independent thought in the social sciences, but this can only emerge when scholars are aware of the broader dynamics in their field and approach their investigations using strategies that consciously resist the habit of conforming to established practices and conventional analyses. The pervasive rationality of the system does have the potential to dominate academic activities, but the ideas of social scientists are not wholly determined by institutional pressures. Autonomous thinking in academia can thrive, provided scholars acknowledge this influence and do what is needed to avoid unwittingly falling in line with institutionally driven conceptual frameworks.[38]

In keeping with this set of concerns, Habermas also reiterated the pragmatists' and critical theorists' critique of positivism and rejected the quest for absolute knowledge about the social world that allegedly transcends all normative foundations.

> The paradigm of the philosophy of consciousness is exhausted. If this is so, the symptoms of exhaustion should dissolve with the transition to the paradigm of mutual understanding.[39]

He suggested that an alternative to the "philosophy of consciousness" can be found in the dynamics of communicative action and in the effort to work toward cooperation and consensus. One way to achieve this, in his view, is to accept the need for common ground in the formation of new knowledge about the social world. He understood the challenges involved in developing mutual understanding in the social sciences and in the public sphere, but he also maintained that striving toward this goal is necessary as a way to prevent the factionalism that can occur in the absence of such an agreement. Building consensus in this context means being willing to reflect on the potential worth of philosophical positions other than one's own. It means thinking about the ways one's personal views may be limited in terms of information and analysis and being open to the possibility of cooperative discussion. Habermas did not depict this course of action as relinquishing one's cherished values, but as considering the potential insight in the positions of others in order to find some measure of agreement and work toward compromise. He viewed this goal as an essential step in bringing together disparate outlooks and in making informed decisions in academia and in society as a whole.[40]

Regarding social research, Habermas conceded that there is a need for more than simply achieving common ground when trying to develop new knowledge about the social world. Finding agreement among scholars regarding a given area of inquiry does not necessarily bring us closer to forming deeper understandings of that area than that which can be achieved through armchair speculation. Instead, he advocated what he called a "pragmatic epistemological realism," where the goal is to operate from a place of mutual understanding while also engaging in empirical inquiry to connect one's analysis to the everyday world. From his point of view, bringing together reasoned discussion and scientific investigation can serve as a valuable way to gain new insight into a particular topic that is both theoretically informed and empirically grounded. Habermas did not contend that such an approach would yield knowledge of an absolute or objective nature, but expressed the position that, although this knowledge is provisional and may change in the future, it is nevertheless of a high caliber when connected to evidence gathered in relation to analyses formed via collective debate and discussion among reflexive and enlightened scholars. He understood that future evidence or new ways of understanding the social issues involved might lead to a shift in these conclusions in the future, but he also argued that the information and analyses developed in this way are of the highest quality possible in the present context.[41]

Habermas did not attempt to separate "pure" thought from the practical factors surrounding its formation. He saw the connections between real-world conditions and collective understanding and knew that social analyses were not free of external forces. In his view, knowledge of the social world is always tied to situational pressures. The goal is then to be aware of these pressures and openly discuss and debate them with one's colleagues, university administrators, and others to help maintain and expand autonomy in the intellectual sphere. Approaching one's work with a sense of the ways situational factors and prevailing cultural norms may be influencing it is, in Habermas' analysis, a crucial first step in striving for intellectual freedom. Consciously addressing these limitations and working to overcome them are essential to the task of bringing new ideas into the domain of social research. Critical thinking thus means actively considering the relationship between institutional pressures and modes of thought. Being cognizant of the ongoing constraints affecting one's work can provide a pathway to ideas that would otherwise be unrealized. This approach enables scholars to move beyond the limitations of conventionally accepted belief and create new analyses. Recognizing the ways practical factors can shape the character of social scientific knowledge is a necessary prerequisite to identifying potential weaknesses in prevailing perspectives and challenging existing dogma. Habermas encouraged scholars to develop a consciousness around these systemic pressures in academia and in the public sphere to help support the goal of independent thought and action on a broad scale.[42]

Habermas' synthesis of ideas helped carry intersubjectivism a long way toward a balanced epistemological orientation for the social sciences. His emphasis on the need for consensus in the construction of new knowledge is tempered by an awareness of the institutional demands facing social scientists as they go about their work. Rather than taking the entirely pessimistic view of the early critical theorists regarding the future directions of modern civilization, he turned to the realm of communication as a possible means of confronting these trends and moving social science toward higher levels of independence in social thought and practice. His appeal to scholars to acknowledge the pressures pushing them toward institutional acquiescence serves as an alternative to the pessimistic position that the fate of knowledge lies in the hands of authoritarian powers. From this vantage point, communicative action can provide a way out of this pattern and endow discussions of social issues with the potential for intellectual autonomy. This shift can then influence the directions of society and help create a foundation for democratic organization in the future.[43]

INTERSUBJECTIVISM

We can see from this brief review of the authors associated with intersubjectivism that they sought to address some of the more pressing challenges involved in learning about the social world. Their emphasis on the interpersonal dimensions of knowledge draws our attention to the ways individual consciousness is connected to the collective beliefs and practices in one's surrounding milieu. Knowledge is, in this sense, an inherently social phenomenon, shaped in part by individual perspectives, but also by cultural norms and traditions and, on a larger sale, institutional and organizational factors. Intersubjectivists argue that while individuals may experience the world in what seems to them to be an intuitive and private manner, there are subtle but strong ties between their own ideas and the established beliefs they have internalized over time through social interaction. The intersubjective orientation brings these dimensions of knowledge to the fore as key components of everyday understanding and as the basis for collective participation in society broadly.

A principal component of this assessment is that the words people use to communicate with one another embody shared meanings that are directly connected to preconceived conceptual frameworks. These agreed-upon understandings help provide the starting assumptions, systems of categorization, and implicit theoretical configurations people routinely use to make sense of the social world and decide how to act in it. While these constructions are learned over time through socialization, they eventually become invisible to the individuals relying on them. To the extent that the bearers of these constructions acknowledge their existence, they are inclined to perceive them as "common sense" or as being tied in some way to a presumed human nature. It is therefore routine, from this perspective, for people to unconsciously adopt and internalize a specific mindset and go through life largely blind to the intersubjective nature of their worldview while, at the same time, being dismissive of those who do not subscribe to their particular way of thinking.

Intersubjectivists point out that this phenomenon applies to social science as well. They maintain that the connection between individual and collective consciousness serves as the basis for the perspectives employed in social research. Intersubjectivism shows us that culturally normative and socially derived ways of making sense of the world provide the conceptual frames social scientists rely on to set up and carry out their investigations. Even those who consider themselves to be operating outside the norms and traditions of mainstream society incorporate ideas they have developed through their own personal interactions into their work. These ideas can be so thoroughly embedded in the recesses of their consciousness that they may fail to see them at all. Rather than operating objectively, as they assume, researchers in this situation draw on ways of making sense of the world that are commonplace in their culture and in their field. This calls into question the idea that social scientific knowledge can be completely neutral and, instead, highlights its intersubjective character.

In addition to focusing on the ways cultural factors shape social research, intersubjectivists express concern regarding the influence of practical factors on this endeavor. From their point of view, institutional dynamics have a significant bearing on the ways social scientists construct and carry out their studies. Whether researchers are facing the expectation that they secure funding from a well-endowed source or the requirement that they frame their projects in line with established convention, the pressures social scientists face as they strive to succeed in their fields are extensive. Intersubjectivists do not claim it is possible to escape the influence of these pressures altogether, but suggest that being cognizant of the ways one's work is tied to institutional expectations is the first step toward intellectual independence. A central goal in this analysis is to recognize these dynamics in order to facilitate a greater degree of autonomy and transcend the boundaries of established thought and practice in one's field.

The emphasis of intersubjectivism on the social dimensions of knowledge provides a way to bring together divergent groups, help them find common ground, and form a collective sense of direction. The concern among inter-subjectivists regarding the potential fragmentation of society leads them to advocate open discussion of social issues, where all parties have a voice in shaping the ideas that rise to the level of legitimate knowledge. Moving in this direction is essential to creating enlightened perspectives and building more interactive, participatory, and democratic forms of political organiza-tion in the present and in the future.

AN ASSESSMENT OF INTERSUBJECTIVISM

This leads us to consider some of the strengths and weaknesses of the inter-subjective orientation as they relate to the social sciences. We can begin this evaluation by pointing out that one of its key strengths is an ability to offer a feasible way to address the need for a starting conceptual apparatus in the formation of new knowledge. Its assertion that there is always a theoretical framework embedded in any investigation and its concern to consciously construct that framework lend intersubjectivism a degree of epistemological competence not present in the positivist orientation. Intersubjectivist scholars recognize the need to establish this starting foundation, and they prioritize the goal of constructing it collectively in order to elevate the quality of their research.

Grounding the ideas of social science in collective understanding also enables researchers to address some of the key issues left unresolved by rela-tivism. Accepting and prioritizing the need for an a priori starting point in the development of new knowledge provides a unique way for social scientists to contend with the contradictions in the paradoxical assertion that truth is a matter of individual perspective. Rather than drift in this direction, the inter-subjective orientation gives researchers the footing they need to meet the prerequisites of social science, including not only a connection to empirical realities but also an awareness of the practical factors involved. Addressing this epistemological challenge opens up a clear pathway to developing theoretically informed and empirically grounded truth claims. The intersub-jectivist practice of seeking truth via a collectively constructed conceptual apparatus offers the means through which to develop new modes of social thought and form innovative and insightful analyses and conclusions.

This raises the question of how the intersubjective orientation compares with that of interpretivism in terms of its ability to guide the directions and framing of social research. We have seen that the interpretive orientation addresses a notable limitation of positivism by acknowledging the need to adopt a conceptual framework when engaging in social research, but we have also observed that it does not resolve the question of how to determine which frames are of a higher caliber than others. Intersubjectivism takes a step in this direction by drawing on the consensus model and considering the influence of interpersonal and institutional factors in shaping the conceptual foundations of social research. From the point of view of authors writing in the intersubjectivist tradition, addressing this issue affords social scientists the opportunity to collectively evaluate a broad array of theoretical frames and identify which of these can best inform their investigations.

In addition to this strength, the intersubjective emphasis on the interpersonal and institutional factors involved in social research helps scholars maintain an awareness of the pressures they face in their respective fields and take the action needed to avoid allowing their studies to fall prey to these potential influences. This provides a way for them to acknowledge the interpretive dimensions of their work while also consciously protecting it from the damage that can be done to it by situational factors.

Although intersubjectivism does indeed take us closer to a balanced epistemological orientation for the social sciences, it is not without its shortcomings. One of the more prevalent criticisms levied against this orientation has to do with its assumptions regarding the possibility of being able to reach consensus in the world of ideas, including in the areas of politics and culture. Critics of intersubjectivism argue that while the notion of consensual agreement is enticing in theory, it is not likely to occur in real life. From the standpoint of this critique, whether one is talking about the contrasting positions of two individuals or of two nations, reality teaches us that the goal of achieving consensus is elusive if not completely unrealizable. Getting to the point where some form of agreement can be attained requires a degree of cooperation that is not feasible in the everyday world. The intersubjective requirement that such a foundation be established calls into question the possibility that this orientation can serve as an epistemological guide for social research.[44]

Another common criticism of intersubjectivism is that its emphasis on building consensus is problematic in that it fails to adequately consider the ways doing so can marginalize alternative perspectives. This suggests that the intersubjectivist stance regarding the need for a starting conceptual foundation requires the holders of divergent perspectives to bend their ideas to fit into the dominant framework and doing so can interfere with the independence of their analyses. Critics of intersubjectivism argue that lesser-known theoretical perspectives may possess an untapped potential to reveal enlightening ways to understand a given area of inquiry, and when these perspectives yield to a dominant conceptual apparatus, they can lose the valuable insight they may have been able to offer in their original form. This means that the ongoing effort to work toward consensus produces frames of knowledge that resonate with existing modes of thought and undermines the legitimacy of views that do not conform to established ways of seeing. Less common perspectives may be pushed aside and relegated to the storage bins of social theory, perhaps to be reevaluated and brought into the mainstream at a later date if the outlook of the larger group happens to shift and opportunities for new ways of thinking arise. From this point of view, the process of building consensus interferes with the autonomy of alternative perspectives and pushes theory in the direction of accepted ways of seeing the world. Critics argue that subscribing to the logic and practice of the intersubjective orientation leads social science down a preset pathway and limits the ability of researchers to think outside the parameters of established convention.

While these criticisms do seem to challenge the core principles of intersubjectivism, they are based on a particular understanding of it that is not necessarily in line with the ideas of its purveyors. Instead of viewing all intersubjectivists as advocating the development of a universal conceptual apparatus to be employed in all instances, we can interpret their position as subscribing to the notion of working toward an agreement to accept a wide range of perspectives in social research. In other words, we can conceive of the intersubjective orientation as suggesting that scholars agree to embrace a diversity of conceptual frameworks and practices in the social sciences and in the social world broadly. Viewing intersubjectivism in this way places it in a vastly different light and gives it a much greater degree of flexibility than originally understood. We can therefore imagine the goal of working toward consensus as a call for an overarching acceptance of a pluralist approach to the development of new knowledge in academia and in society.

One point that must be raised in this regard is that establishing a pluralist arrangement in the realm of social thought requires some agreement among the various participants to do so. Pluralism is not something that emerges spontaneously or survives on its own. It only comes into being and endures as the result of a conscious effort on the part of those involved to abide by the parameters of such a system. One of the interesting characteristics of pluralist thought is that there is both an acceptance of multiple perspectives and an intolerance for perspectives that require the squelching of others. It is an integral feature of pluralism to rely on an agreement among all parties to abide by the philosophy of live and let live. This is not the product of a lack of agreement in the world of ideas, but one that is grounded in mutual understanding regarding the accepted rules of collective participation.

Another key response to these criticisms is that the consensus approach to the development of knowledge is already being used in many contexts, both within and outside academia. In the social sciences, for instance, the system of peer review serves as a way to assess the quality of manuscripts on a routine basis. Requesting the input of colleagues in one's field to gauge the caliber of work submitted for publication involves relying on a collective evaluation rather than on a universal set of standards to be applied in all instances. The existence of a variety of journals, books, and other forms of media in social science employs the vetting process of peer review while also providing the opportunity for a range of perspectives to exist simultaneously. The inherently interpretive character of social scientific knowledge has led to an extensive proliferation of perspectives in each field. Drawing on peer review and embracing a diversity of outlets serve as a way to allow several perspectives to flourish while also setting standards for what constitutes high-quality research. The evaluation process is not simply a matter of appraising the empirical validity of claims embedded in the manuscript. It involves considering the ways these findings are put together conceptually to ascertain whether they are in line with the prevailing thinking and beliefs about truth and validity that exist in the field generally and among the scholars associated with that publication. In this sense, the intersubjective approach has helped address the problems of interpretation as they relate to matters of truth in the social sciences.

It should be pointed out that referring to the system of peer review does not in itself fully address the concern that the intersubjective quest for mutual understanding can restrict outlooks that stray from the mainstream of social thought and practice. There are plenty of instances where reviewers favor one set of theoretical perspectives and methodological approaches over others and reject research that does not resonate with their preferred views. When this happens, authors may turn to alternative journals and other forms of media to share their analyses and conclusions, but one can argue that publishing in lesser-known outlets sends a message to the social science community that these writings are not as valuable or as important as those published in mainstream journals or in major presses. The system of peer review can thus provide a degree of favoritism toward established modes of thought and practice in each field and reinforce conventional analyses and methodologies. Understood this way, we see that an arrangement of this nature does not fully circumvent the limitations of convention and may, in fact, lead to the ongoing reproduction of accepted norms in social research, relegating innovative work to less prominent outlets and undermining the potential for uniquely insightful analyses and conclusions to reach a wider readership.

Viewing intersubjectivism as advocating the development of a range of perspectives addresses the critique that the quest for mutual understanding excludes views that do not fit into the rubric of a dominant theoretical framework, but it raises new issues for the epistemology of social science.

Adopting a pluralist reading of the intersubjective orientation leads us to ask new questions about the boundaries of social research. Does the acceptance of a range of ideas revive the dilemmas of relativism and facilitate the prolif-eration of an endless stream of perspectives with no way to determine their validity, or does it offer a way out of this dilemma? If the answer is to set boundaries for these perspectives, how might social scientists establish these boundaries? What criteria can they use to do so? Is it necessary to establish any limitations at all or is it preferable to avoid setting the parameters for what is considered high-quality social research? While understanding the intersubjective orientation in this light does unleash new epistemological pos-sibilities, it opens a Pandora's box of potential problems as well.

Intersubjectivists are inclined to acknowledge the normative character of social research, but also take the position that the solution to this dilemma can be attained by collectively setting standards through deliberation and discussion. The goal is to consciously construct an environment where a multiplicity of ideas can flourish while also relying on a specific set of criteria to assess the quality of the social research involved. The intersubjectivist call for mutual understanding can thus be seen as a willingness to consider the potential worth of perspectives other than one's own while also encouraging the production of empirically grounded, innovative, and insightful analyses and conclusions. Viewing intersubjectivism in this way is not a renunciation of the effort to establish the characteristics of high-quality social inquiry. It is a conscious decision to facilitate a range of perspectives while also working collectively toward agreement among members in the social science commu-nity regarding the standards that inform the field as a whole.

This raises the question of whether or not intersubjectivism effectively addresses the connections between knowledge and power. Critics argue that this orientation fails to adequately theorize these connections and instead assumes it is possible to develop ideas independently of institutional pres-sures. The basis of this criticism is that the notion of open discussion and debate is grounded in the assumption that people are somehow able to tran-scend practical pressures and think and act in ways that do not succumb to the realities of conventional knowledge production. From this point of view, there are so many factors influencing worldview—media, family, education, occupational expectations, peers, and others—that the effort to move beyond them is unrealistic and out of touch with practical reality.[45]

A counterargument to this position is that the intersubjective orientation is actually one that has focused specifically on the connections between power and knowledge from its inception. When looking at the foundational thinkers of intersubjectivism, we can see that their ideas are grounded in a concern to address the ways institutions and social conventions relate to individual consciousness. They have consistently theorized the ties between practical factors and the prevailing forms of knowledge in various social contexts. Habermas, in particular, noted an ongoing decline in the quality of public discussion and debate and characterized this as being connected to the overwhelming impact of structural influences.[46] The focus of this group on the nexus between society and the individual has, in large part, served as the basis for intersubjectivism on the whole.

While the purveyors of this orientation recognize the challenges involved in confronting established belief, they do not assume that the dominant structural factors in a given setting determine how people think and act. From an intersubjective point of view, knowledge does not simply grow out of a set of social conditions but emerges in relation to the unique constructions people create in the midst of those conditions. It is common for people to develop new ideas and share these with others to the point where they eventually become more widely accepted on a societal level. Intersubjective scholars characterize the development of new perspectives as being connected to the practical experiences people have in their own lives—including those that do not resonate with institutional frames. From this vantage point, people develop their worldviews relationally and continue to retain the potential for independent thought. Original modes of understanding can emerge spontaneously and in forms that do not match the logic of everyday convention. This is how, even in an institutionally dominated world, communicative action can serve as a countervailing force to structural pressures and infuse innovative ideas into the domain of public consciousness.[47]

Intersubjectivism has faced significant challenges throughout the course of its history, but it has managed to address these challenges in thought-provoking ways. The focus of its practitioners on the connections between social environment and individual consciousness provides a balanced way to shed new light on the everyday realities of contemporary social life. Their emphasis on working toward mutual understanding in the formation of new knowledge draws attention to the importance in establishing a common grounding for social research. Offering a way to construct and maintain that grounding is a unique feature of this orientation and a key development in the philosophy of social science. Although intersubjectivism does have its shortcomings, it nevertheless serves as a valuable stepping-stone in the development of a balanced and theoretically informed epistemological orientation for the social sciences.

NOTES

1. Husserl discusses the intersubjective nature of experience in: Edmund Husserl, *Ideas Pertaining to a Pure Phenomenology and to a Phenomenological Philosophy*

– *Second Book: Studies in the Phenomenology of Constitution*, trans. Richard Rojcewicz and André Schuwer (Dordrecht: Kluwer, 2000; orig. pub. 1913–1928), 90–95.

2. Schütz discusses this phenomenon in: *Alfred Schütz: Collected Papers II, Studies in Social Theory*, ed. Arvid Brodersen (The Hague: Martinus Nijhoff, 1976; orig. pub. 1964).

3. For more on this position, please see: Schütz, "Common-Sense and Scientific Interpretation," 1–38.

4. Husserl discusses this in: *Ideas – First Book*, 3–27 and 369–81. Schütz discusses this point in: "Common-Sense and Scientific Interpretation," 7–14.

5. For more on Peirce's background, please see: Joseph Brent, *Charles Sanders Peirce: A Life* (Bloomington, IN: Indiana University Press, 1998).

6. Peirce discusses this in: Charles Sanders Peirce, "How to Make Our Ideas Clear," in *The Essential Peirce, Volume 1*, ed. N. Houser and C. Kloesel (Bloomington, IN: Indiana University Press, 1992; orig. pub. 1878), 124–41.

7. Peirce, "How to Make Our Ideas Clear," 124–41.

8. Charles Sanders Peirce, *The Collected Papers of Charles Sanders Peirce, Volumes 1–6*, ed. Charles Hartshorne and Paul Weiss (Cambridge, MA: Harvard University Press, 1931–1935), *Volumes 7–8*, ed. Arthur W. Burks (Cambridge, MA: Harvard University Press, 1958), CP 1.591, CP 2.96.

9. Peirce, *The Collected Papers*, CP 2.102.

10. This quote is taken from: Peirce, *The Collected Papers*, CP 5.9.

11. Peirce, *The Collected Papers*, CP 5.1–5.404.

12. James discusses the connections between experience and truth in: Chapter IV, "The Relation Between Knower and Known," in *The Meaning of Truth: A Sequel to 'Pragmatism'* (Adelaide, Australia: University of Adelaide Press, 2014; orig. pub. 1909).

13. James, *The Meaning of Truth*.

14. For more on this position, please see: William James, *Pragmatism: A New Name for Some Old Ways of Thinking* (Adelaide, Australia: University of Adelaide Press, 2014; orig. pub. 1907).

15. This quote is from a diary entry of James, published in: Ralph Barton Perry, *The Thought and Character of William James* (Nashville, TN: Vanderbilt University Press, 1996), 323.

16. James outlined this position in an address to the Philosophical Union at Berkeley on August 26, 1898. This address was published as: William James, "Philosophical Conceptions and Practical Results," *University Chronicle* 1, no. 4 (September 1898).

17. James, "The Meaning of the Word Truth," *The Meaning of Truth*.

18. James, *The Meaning of Truth*.

19. For more on this, please see: Dewey, "Eclipse of the Public"; John Dewey, *The Public and Its Problems* (Chicago, IL: Swallow, 1954).

20. Dewey, "Search for the Great Community," *The Public and Its Problems*, 143–84.

21. Dewey, "Search for the Great Community," *The Public and Its Problems*, 143–84.

22. Dewey, "Search for the Public," *The Public and Its Problems*, 8–36.

23. Dewey, "The Democratic State," *The Public and Its Problems*, 75–109.

24. Dewey, "The Problem of Method," *The Public and Its Problems*, 185–220.

25. For more on this, please see: Richard Bernstein, *The Pragmatic Turn* (Cambridge, UK: Polity Press, 2010).

26. For a clear depiction of the epistemological perspective of critical theory, please see: Anastasia Marinopoulou, *Critical Theory and Epistemology: The Politics of Modern Thought and Science* (Manchester: Manchester University Press, 2017).

27. The Institute for Social Research was affiliated with Goethe University in Frankfurt. It was created in 1923, but then it was closed down by the Nazis in 1933. For more information about the institute and the development of critical theory, please see: Robert Antonio, "The Origin, Development, and Contemporary Status of Critical Theory," *The Sociological Quarterly* 24, no. 3 (Summer, 1983): 325–51.

28. Max Horkheimer and Theodor Adorno outlined this view in their book, *Dialectic of Enlightenment*, trans. John Cumming (New York, NY: Continuum Publishing, 1993).

29. Please see: Max Horkheimer and Theodor Adorno, "The Culture Industry," in *Dialectic of Enlightenment*, trans. John Cumming (New York, NY: Continuum Publishing, 1993).

30. Horkheimer and Adorno, *Dialectic of Enlightenment*.

31. Horkheimer and Adorno, *Dialectic of Enlightenment*.

32. Although the pessimism exhibited in the work of the early critical theorists may seem extreme on the surface, one can hopefully understand the origins of this sentiment, given the unique nature of their experience at the time of their writing. It should be noted that these authors did step back a bit from their initial pessimism toward modern society after World War II and conceded the existence of some measure of hope for civilization to move in a favorable direction. For further information on this change, please see: Antonio, "The Origin, Development, and Contemporary Status of Critical Theory."

33. One of the more comprehensive works written by Habermas on this topic is: Jürgen Habermas, *The Philosophical Discourse of Modernity*, trans. F. Lawrence (Cambridge, MA: MIT Press, 1992).

34. Habermas, *The Philosophical Discourse of Modernity*.

35. Habermas outlines this view in: Jürgen Habermas, *The Structural Transformation of the Public Sphere: An Inquiry into a Category of Bourgeois Society*, trans. Thomas Burger (Cambridge, MA: The MIT Press, 1991; orig. pub. 1962).

36. Habermas actually called these "knowledge constitutive interests." Please see: Jürgen Habermas, *Knowledge and Human Interests*, trans. Jeremy Shapiro (Boston, MA: Beacon Press, 1971).

37. For a more in-depth description of this view, please see: Jürgen Habermas, *The Theory of Communicative Action: Reason and the Rationalization of Society, Volume 1*, trans. Thomas McCarthy (Boston, MA: Beacon, 1985).

38. Habermas presents this view in: Jürgen Habermas, *The Theory of Communicative Action: Lifeworld and System: A Critique of Functionalist Reason, Volume 2*, trans. Thomas McCarthy (Boston, MA: Beacon, 1985).

39. Habermas, *The Philosophical Discourse of Modernity*, 296.

40. Habermas, *The Philosophical Discourse of Modernity*.

41. Habermas, *The Theory of Communicative Action*.

42. Habermas, *Knowledge and Human Interests*.

43. Habermas, *The Theory of Communicative Action*.

44. One example of this form of critique can be found in: Lasse Thomassen, *Deconstructing Habermas* (London, UK: Routledge, 2008).

45. An extensive collection of essays evaluating Habermas' ideas of intersubjectivity can be found in: Jürgen Habermas, *Habermas: Critical Debates*, ed. John B. Thompson and David Held (London: MacMillan, 1982).

46. Habermas, *The Structural Transformation of the Public Sphere*.

47. Habermas discusses these ideas in *The Theory of Communicative Action*.

Chapter 5

A Balanced Epistemological Orientation for the Social Sciences

At this point in our discussion, we can draw on the lessons of these evaluations to work toward the larger goal of outlining the characteristics of a balanced epistemological orientation for the social sciences. We have seen that positivism, relativism, interpretivism, and intersubjectivism collectively offer an array of valuable contributions to our understanding of social phenomena, but also that they each possess certain weaknesses that interfere with their potential to serve as an epistemological guide for social research. Our goal in this regard is to draw on these strong points while avoiding their shortcomings to build an epistemological orientation that is balanced and theoretically informed. The following is an overview of that orientation.

THE POSITIVIST SPIRIT

The first and most significant characteristic of a balanced epistemological orientation for the social sciences is an acceptance of the inherent value of the positivist spirit. We refer to the positivist spirit in this context as a desire to understand people in a variety of social environments and over the course of time, from the individual to society as a whole. Abiding by this spirit means embracing the goal of seeking to learn more about all aspects of the social world, including not only people's behavior but also the meanings associated with that behavior and the broader societal conditions in place that support it. This involves studying the ways belief systems and cultural practices interrelate with one another in the development of contemporary realities. It also involves studying the past as a way to learn more about the present and develop a sense of where society may be headed in the future if existing trends do not change. Positivism does have its share of problems, but its underlying spirit is worth keeping and developing further, especially if we conceive of it as a passion to cultivate deeper insight into all forms of social phenomena.

Subsumed within the auspices of this first characteristic is an awareness of the value of critique in social scientific analysis. Embracing the positivist spirit means adopting a skeptical attitude with regard to any and all truth claims. It requires social scientists to view statements about social phenomena with a critical eye and an inclination toward doubt. This entails engaging in extensive questioning to reveal the potential inconsistencies, conceptual contradictions, and other inadequacies that may be embedded in various truth claims and in the ways of thinking supporting those claims. Approaching social research in this light means being willing to expose the unstated assumptions in all social analyses and search for hidden gaps in one line of argumentation or another. The motive for this practice is not to blindly tear down the work of others, leaving no alternatives in place, but to improve the quality of social science overall. In fostering a skeptical attitude, the element of critique in the positivist spirit provides a solid starting point in our effort to build a balanced epistemology for the social sciences.

PERSPECTIVE

This leads us to the second fundamental characteristic of a balanced orientation, and that is a willingness to acknowledge the point that all facets of social science—research, teaching, writing, public speaking, and so on—are carried out in relation to a particular conceptual apparatus. There is no getting around the fact that social scientists employ culturally normative frameworks in making sense of the various aspects of the social world they seek to understand. Accepting this basic premise means coming to terms with the role of perspective in shaping the ways social scientific analyses are conceived, constructed, carried out, and communicated to others.

Viewing social science in this way means balancing the drive to learn about the social world with an awareness of its interpretive dimensions. It means approaching the task of social research rigorously while also being cognizant of the culturally specific ways investigators construct their subject matter. The interpretive nature of social research does not render it unable to shed new light on everyday realities. Although it is always grounded in a particular set of norms and traditions, it can nevertheless expose the fallacy of unsubstantiated myth and facilitate the development of perceptive ways to comprehend the social world. It can help us learn more about groups of people outside our immediate milieu and illuminate phenomena that would otherwise be invisible to the casual observer. The theoretical perspectives inherent in any research project certainly condition its findings, but acknowledging this fact does not lead us to the conclusion that these findings are necessarily flawed. Viewing social science from a balanced epistemological orientation means accepting its perspectival foundations while also acknowledging its ability to produce enlightening analyses and conclusions.

It is also important to point out that accepting the interpretive nature of social science does not suggest the position that reality is simply what one makes it out to be. Being aware of the epistemological subtleties of social research means having the capacity to differentiate between the interpretivist idea that social scientific knowledge exists in relation to a particular conceptual apparatus and the relativist notion that truth is in the eye of the beholder. Interpretive scholars seek to understand social phenomena and share these accounts with others in interactive ways to facilitate the development of new knowledge. Relativists are inclined to avoid making truth claims of any sort and instead offer implicit ideas without a firm commitment regarding the connections of these claims to empirical reality. Whereas interpretivists strive to better understand the social world, relativists focus on the internal contradictions in one mode of thought or another, without offering much in the way of substantive alternatives. Approaching social research from a balanced epistemological orientation means being aware of its constructed nature while also working toward an insightful portrayal of the particular area of social life one is studying.

Many social scientists are uncomfortable with imprecision. This is understandable because, after all, a central component of their mission is to bring clarity to what is happening in the social world. In their effort to be precise, they often construct systems of investigation that are, at times, capable of producing very clear factual information on a given topic. In other instances, however, these same systems offer only a partial image of the reality they seek to understand. Adopting a balanced approach to the social sciences means being conscious of this issue while also being willing to delve into topics that involve some degree of uncertainty and are therefore likely to yield murky results. It is crucial from within this orientation to avoid being deterred by the expectation to always generate infallible conclusions. Succumbing to this expectation can lead researchers to shy away from challenging topics and leave broad segments of the social world unexamined and, therefore, less well-understood. The goal from a balanced epistemological orientation—one that recognizes the inexact nature of social research—is to learn more about social phenomena that would be largely unknown and unappreciated without this type of inquiry. Studies carried out in this manner may not yield incontrovertible results, but they can tell us something about the social world that would have remained hidden without them.

VALUES

This brings us to a discussion of the third characteristic of a balanced epistemological orientation for the social sciences, and that is an acceptance of
the place of values in all social scientific analyses. It is understood from this
orientation that researchers are capable of shedding new light on their topic of
study when they minimize the presence of values in their investigations, but
it is also understood that it is not possible to fully eliminate the influence of
values altogether. This means that researchers can enhance the quality of their
work by diminishing the role of values in their investigations while, at the
same time, balancing this effort with an awareness that values are an inherent
part of all social research.

The apparent contradiction in the above assertion is easily addressed when
considering the example of a common value held by social scientists—
namely the pursuit of truth. As we have seen in earlier chapters of this book,
the pursuit of truth is itself a value-laden endeavor. Many social scientists
seeking to learn about a given topic believe themselves to be operating in a
neutral manner, where they are simply collecting facts and forming objective
analyses and conclusions about these facts to share with others. Presenting
researchers with the question of why they are engaged in this activity is likely
to yield a response that the answer is obvious and that there is no need to get
involved in such frivolous discussions. From their point of view, they are
doing it to better understand what is going on in that particular domain of
the social world—that is all. To those outside the profession, however, this
endeavor may seem odd and difficult to comprehend. Why would someone
spend so much of their lives inundated in this kind of work when they could
be doing other, more interesting activities? The answer, of course, is that
social scientists value the insight that research and analysis can bring and,
in this sense, they value the pursuit of truth. Recognizing this connection
shows us that the endeavor of social research involves minimizing certain
values while also operating in a value-laden manner. Social science is never
value-free, but when we strive to limit the influence of values that have the
potential to restrict our understanding while also remaining cognizant of our
own social scientific values, we can enhance our understanding of social reality and make strides toward high-caliber research.[1]

A second integral value of social science is reason. Although reason has
its own limitations, it nevertheless provides the basis for critical thinking
in social science in a variety of ways. An obvious example of this can be
found in the need to differentiate between causation and association. Seeing
two variables in a given context shift in conjunction with one another can
lead some to mistakenly assume that changes in one are causing changes in
the other. Placing a value on reason helps keep these kinds of assumptions

in check and expose possible flaws in less well-thought-out assessments. Reason is valued in social science because it enables researchers to work toward clarity in their investigations and to address the challenges involved in seeking to understand the social world. It is at the core of their decisions about what to focus on, how to frame their inquiry, and how to discuss what they have learned with others. Reason is thus an essential element of social science from start to finish.[2]

Having said this, it is also important to acknowledge that conceptions of reason can vary from one perspective to another. What may seem to be perfectly reasonable from one vantage point can appear as complete folly from another. The observation that social scientists rely on reason in their analyses does not mean they are impervious to any flaws in their thinking whatsoever. Divergent perceptions among social scientists on a given topic often lead to different analyses, even though members in each camp may consider themselves to be approaching their work in a reasonable manner. These differences, however, do not lead us to the conclusion that the use of reason is completely ineffectual in helping social scientists evaluate each other's arguments. Approaching this issue from a balanced epistemological orientation means recognizing the value of reason while also being aware of its normative dimensions.

A third basic value employed in the social sciences is having a sense of the importance of individual freedom. Embracing freedom as a value can be challenging because it means considering the possibility that strengthening the freedoms of some may actually impede those of others. It also means being aware of the potential of social science to further rationalize society and diminish the ability of individuals to shape their own fate. Embracing freedom as a value of the social sciences means consciously pushing back against pressures that are designed to engineer the social order in a mechanistic manner, even when the intention is to improve it. It is not in the domain of social science to lead people down one preset pathway or another, particularly when doing so can have the effect of repressing their desires, directing their ways of thinking, or managing their actions. A central goal of social science is to engage in research with an eye toward individual freedom and an interest in enabling people to have as much leeway as possible in deciding how to live their lives.[3]

At the same time, the potential of social science to illuminate social reality must be tempered with an awareness that the people being studied may have some degree of insight into their own situations that the researchers themselves do not understand. This is why it is crucial for social scientists to adopt an interactive approach in their work, learning about the experiences of others while also communicating what they have gleaned from their investigations. Their goal is less a matter of unilaterally presenting conclusions to members of the broader population than it is one of engaging in ongoing discussions that involve teaching and learning each step of the way.

Approaching social science from a balanced epistemological orientation thus means accepting the fundamental values of truth, reason, and freedom. It means seeking to develop thorough understandings of social phenomena while also taking into consideration the impact of one's actions on individuals, groups, and society as a whole. Social scientists do value the pursuit of truth, but they do not abide by this value in an isolated or single-minded fashion. Their task in this regard is to remain committed to learning more about the social world while also being aware of the ways their values interrelate with one another and the potential consequences their actions may bring.

THE POWER/KNOWLEDGE NEXUS

Discussing these issues leads us to the fourth major characteristic of a balanced epistemological orientation, and that is being cognizant of the connections between practical pressures, power dynamics, and the dominant perspectives social scientists employ in their work. Social research does not take place in a vacuum, but is always carried out in a particular context, with conditions that yield specific opportunities and constraints. These contextual factors can influence the ways researchers construct their investigations, develop their assessments, and communicate their findings to others. Operating from a balanced epistemological orientation means being aware of these factors and understanding how they are connected to social scientific practices and perspectives.

What are some of the pressures researchers face on a regular basis and how do these relate to the theoretical fames they use? Are they able to approach their work independently in the face of these pressures? To what extent do practical constraints influence their analyses of the topics they study? How do these factors relate to the perspectives they convey to others? These are among the fundamental questions of the field as a whole. How researchers choose to respond to these questions has a significant bearing on the knowledge they develop and disseminate. Being conscious of the connections between practical factors and the world of ideas is a necessary first step in addressing these issues and in maintaining a measure of autonomy in their work.

An example of this kind of influence can be found in the quest for career success. There are quite a few rather intense expectations placed on new scholars as they strive to establish themselves in academia. Graduate students typically work hard to gain the respect of their more established colleagues. This dynamic is significant in terms of its potential to socialize them into the culture of their field. A common practice in this milieu is for graduate students to be invited to work collaboratively with their professors as research assistants. Doing so is generally a great opportunity, and few in their position would allow it to pass by unaccepted. Such an approach is reasonable in that it facilitates a mentoring relationship that provides them with the guidance they need to become familiar with the practices of their new profession.

An issue that arises in conjunction with this tradition is that the prevailing perspectives in an area of inquiry may be uncritically passed down from one generation of scholars to the next. Experienced professors involved in this relationship are inclined to draw on the ways of thinking they have grown accustomed to over years of working on a particular topic. The frames they employ may be so deeply embedded in their minds, in their research projects, and in the ideas they communicate that they have come to see them as given. These frames are typically connected to the literature in their field and reinforced by an abundance of data supporting them. It is not the position of graduate students in these instances to question them or reconfigure them on the basis of their own habits of thought. Instead, their job is to carry out the tasks assigned to them by their mentors. Graduate students who wish to be successful in these situations do what is expected of them. This helps them garner the approval they need to move forward with their careers.

Throughout the course of this process, graduate students learn how to see the issues being studied and incorporate these perspectives into their own work. They often choose to write their dissertations and publish articles on these same topics, carrying forward the ideas they have learned from their mentors while assisting them. Over time, if they are successful, they may develop a reputation as scholars who are well versed in the areas of research they studied in graduate school. Once they become professionals in their particular field, they are likely to work with their own graduate students who may then draw on these frames and carry them forward in the future. As these ideas make their way from one generation of scholars to the next, the potential for creative thinking and innovative analysis can decline. New developments taking place in society may then be missed or poorly understood when attempting to understand them on the basis of ideas formed in an earlier time.

Clearly, not all professors and graduate students enter into this kind of relationship. Being aware of this phenomenon may lead some faculty members to provide their students with a bit of leeway in their thought processes and encourage them to develop their own ways of framing the topics they study. This is an example of approaching one's work from a balanced epistemological orientation—maintaining an awareness of the potentially limiting consequences of connecting students to preset ways of thinking and, instead, finding a middle ground between the need to assert one's own view and a willingness to yield to their less experienced, but perhaps more insightful ways of interpreting the phenomena at hand. Not all students have the analytical prowess to take on this challenge, of course, and in these instances, it is certainly in their best interest for the professor to guide them more closely. However, unless professors adopt a flexible approach in their mentoring responsibilities, the potential of younger scholars to develop qualitatively new forms of analysis may be lost.

Another contextual factor shaping the directions and character of social science can be found in the requirement that scholars narrow the focus of their work to become specialists in a particular area of research. The tendency toward specialization in the social sciences is valuable because it enables researchers to dig deeply into their areas of interest and come up with detailed information regarding the aspects of the social world they are studying. At the same time, this practice can interfere with their ability to maintain a sense of the connections between these details and factors outside this circumscribed domain. While specialization does produce an abundance of knowledge about a certain area of social life, it can also limit the potential of researchers to understand the ties between their subject matter and the broader dynamics that are a part of it.

Given that a central goal of social science is to develop perspicacious understandings of the social order and that specialization enables researchers to dig more deeply into their topics of interest, one way to address this issue is to seek a balance between each of these two requirements. Operating from a balanced epistemological orientation on this matter means not only striving to forge in-depth interpretations of one's area of interest, but to study this area in relation to its connections to the social whole. It means being willing to construct analyses on this topic that bridge the divide between specialized accounts and those that examine it from a more expansive point of view. Doing so entails being familiar with the literature in one's area of specialization while also having knowledge of the literature addressing the relationship between this area and the larger social forces of which it is a part—to the extent that the latter exists at all. Every area of research in the social sciences, no matter how isolated, has some ties to the events and trends surrounding it. Adopting a balanced approach in this endeavor means being willing to specialize while also maintaining an awareness of the connections between the local and societal factors involved.

This leads us to a third contextual factor influencing the nature and directions of social research, and that is the requirement that scholars obtain external funding for their projects in order to survive and thrive in the field. It is understood that social research typically requires some measure of funding to be carried out effectively. Whether investigators seek to understand the psychological states of individuals on a personal level or the beliefs and actions of groups of people on a grand scale, the need for research funding is ever present. Some questions that arise in this regard are: To what extent does this requirement motivate researchers to modify the frames they employ in their work to suit the expectations of potential funders? If shifts of this sort are taking place, what is their cumulative impact on the nature and directions of social research? How can social scientists retain the flexibility they need to independently guide the directions and framing of their investigations?

Reflecting on these questions leads us to consider the possibility that the research frames being used in these contexts may differ from those that would become salient in the absence of any funding requirements. There are obviously times when the ideals of researchers and funding organizations coincide with one another and where the issues involved are of concern to a vast segment of the social science community. In these instances, it is less likely that the demand for external funding has any limiting effects on the kinds of projects being studied or on the ways these studies are designed and carried out. However, in cases where these do not coincide, the potential for frames to shift in relation to the goals of funding organizations can be more pronounced. Under these circumstances, the original ways of framing the issues may be altered significantly or extinguished entirely. When this happens, the independence of researchers can be compromised along with their ability to develop new insight into the phenomena they are studying.

Individual scholars engaged in small-scale interpersonal research may be able to work on their own and operate on the basis of independent perspectives, but the requirements of larger social research projects generally undermine the broader feasibility of the lone-wolf approach. The question that arises from this conundrum is how researchers wishing to engage in large-scale projects can obtain the support they need without having to reconfigure their ideas to satisfy potential funders.

One way to do this is to encourage the development of institutions that are not connected to any political or economic interests other than those involving the effort to better understand social phenomena. It is crucial in this context to recognize the value of institutions that are capable of supporting independent scholarship. This is nothing new, and one can point to examples where universities, professional associations, and other organizations have, at times, managed to provide this kind of support. We know this is possible because it has been done. The goal, in this sense, is to strengthen the effort to expand avenues through which social scientists can operate independently and work toward their objectives without having to cater to the expectations of potential funders.[4]

While it is important to be critical of conventional thinking, we must also acknowledge that there are instances where the dominant perspectives in a given field may be among the more enlightened analyses available when compared to the alternatives proposed. The key point to stress in this regard is that alternatives to convention are not necessarily superior to established frames of analysis. At times, prevailing modes of thought do have strengths that alternatives do not share, and it would be rather dogmatic of us to assume that unconventional perspectives are always more telling than the conventional variety. The goal from a balanced epistemological orientation is to avoid predetermining the relative worth of any theoretical perspective and, instead, openly assess all analyses, regardless of their position in the hierarchy of established belief.

There are many other examples of the ways contextual factors have the potential to shape the directions of social science, but rather than attempt to list them all here, suffice it to say that, from a balanced epistemological orientation, the goal is to develop insightful understandings of social phenomena and to do so with an awareness that this can best be accomplished by approaching one's work independently. Being cognizant of these contextual factors is a necessary precursor to developing high-quality social science. Without this awareness, researchers may be prone to succumbing to these factors and inadvertently allowing their frames to shift as a result. Operating from a balanced epistemological orientation means being conscious of these dynamics and taking the steps needed to avoid succumbing to them. Doing so provides a way to create new analyses and make progress toward fulfilling the promise of social science.

REFLEXIVITY

Thinking about the influence of practical pressures on the directions of social science provides the foundation for our discussion of the fifth characteristic of a balanced epistemological orientation, and that is understanding the crucial role of reflexivity in social research. Social scientists have observed throughout the course of history that there are strong ties between the social location of a particular group of people and the predominant ideas, beliefs, and practices of that group. We also know that what is seen as "common sense" from the point of view of one culture may be thought of as strange or counterintuitive from that of another. Approaching social research reflexively means applying this bit of insight to social scientists themselves to identify the ways their own social locations and life experiences connect to the ideas, beliefs, and practices they employ in their research. What are some of the culturally specific norms and traditions researchers abide by in their investigations? How are these connected to their understandings of the topics they study? The goal of reflexivity is to gain a deeper awareness of these factors in order to see how the a priori assumptions of social scientists shape the kinds of analyses they develop. It involves becoming cognizant of their own under-lying belief systems and reflecting on these as they go about the endeavor of trying to understand others.[5]

Approaching the task of social research reflexively can yield a variety of outcomes, depending on the insight investigators derive from this process. In some instances, thinking about their own cultural background can lead researchers to the realization that their perspectives are somewhat limited and may be interfering with their ability to understand the phenomena they are studying. Developing this awareness can inspire them to reevaluate these ideas and possibly revise or replace them with alternatives that broaden their purview and offer new pathways to developing insightful analyses of the issues they address.

In other instances, adopting a reflexive attitude may suggest that their life experiences and preexisting assumptions about the social world provide a unique level of insight into the individuals or groups they are studying and they may choose, as a result, to retain their initial perspective and perhaps develop it further to elevate the quality of their research. Drawing on the prin-ciples of reflexivity in this way creates an avenue through which research-ers can enhance their awareness of their own conceptual framework and strengthen their analyses overall.

At this point in our discussion, it is appropriate to consider standpoint theory and its connections to reflexivity as they relate to social research. Standpoint theory overlaps with the concept of reflexivity in that it also focuses on the ways the backgrounds and life experiences of social scientists play a part in shaping their worldviews and the perspectives they employ in their work. The purveyors of standpoint theory go a bit further, however, and argue that the quest for objectivity characteristic of the social sciences can lead researchers to overlook the inherent subjectivities of everyday life and form analyses that are stilted as a result. These subjectivities are at the core of what makes us human and constitute an inherent element of the phenomena social scientists seek to understand. Filtering out these aspects of the social world can have the unintended consequence of leaving researchers with mis-guided assessments of the topics they claim to know so well.[6]

Standpoint theorists also argue that it is preferable for researchers to not only be conscious of the relationship between the contextual factors inform-ing their worldviews and the directions of their research, but to present this information explicitly as integral components of their investigations. The logic of this position is that all social scientists have vantage points from which they view their subject matter and, since this is the case, it is mislead-ing to communicate their findings without mentioning this integral compo-nent of their inquiry. Standpoint theorists argue that the positivist approach can paint a false image of social scientists as completely neutral observers when the reality is that they are not. In failing to overtly state the ways their backgrounds, interests, and perspectives factor into the selection and framing their research, they leave out aspects of the issues involved that would help others better grasp where they are coming from and how they formed their ideas. Bringing this information into the presentation of their work can contribute to the goals of social science by offering a more open and honest approach to social research and fostering deeper and more insightful understandings of the social phenomena being studied.[7]

Some social scientists may think of their own work as having attained such a high level of objectivity that there is no need for them to consider reflexivity as an option. The reality, of course, is that these social scientists are human beings and, as such, cannot deny that they are situated in a particular context, rely on a conceptual framework, and embrace a specific set of ideas about their work. Even a casual review of past journals over an extended period of time reveals the perspectival shifts that can occur from one generation of scholars to the next on a topic of study. Yet, those operating from within the logic of a specific perspective in a given time period nevertheless manage to somehow convince themselves that they are independent of any such influences. Being reflexive does not mean thinking about this issue briefly and continuing on with one's research in an uncritical fashion. It means making the effort to be conscious of any unspoken or unrealized assumptions one may have and addressing these to raise the caliber of social scientific research on the whole.

SCIENTIFIC AND POLITICAL KNOWLEDGE

This brings us to the sixth characteristic of a balanced epistemological orientation for the social sciences, and that is having an awareness of the differences between the ethics of science and those of politics. As we discussed earlier, a central goal of social science is to seek thorough understandings of the social world from the level of the individual to society as a whole. When approaching social research in conjunction with the ethics of science, investigators may hypothesize about what they expect to find or they may develop research questions to guide their inquiry, but they do not tailor their study to favor a preset conclusion. Instead, they genuinely seek to learn more about their areas of investigation and contribute to the development of broadminded analyses on this topic.

In contrast to this approach, social scientists embracing the ethics of politics engage in social research to support a specific political agenda. This can be seen as working toward the development of political knowledge. According to this way of thinking, social scientists have a responsibility to operate in a prescriptive manner because doing so can push back against the injustices, absurdities, and harmful trends unfolding in the social order. Embracing this perspective means adopting an advocacy position with regard to one's area of study to address pressing social problems and potentially change society for the better. From this point of view, social scientists have a responsibility to promote a predetermined set of political goals because failing to do so may open the door to competing analyses and diminish the opportunity for positive social change.

In addition, scholars operating in relation to the ethics of politics are inclined to argue that mainstream social scientific analyses tend to reinforce establishmentarian perspectives and preserve the status quo—even when that status quo may be unjust, wrongheaded, or corrupt. Their position is that traditional scholarship has a greater potential to support officially sanctioned views and unwittingly reinforce oppressive ways of looking at social issues, leaving little room for innovative or liberating analyses. According to scholars in this camp, using one's work to promote a preset political agenda can have a positive influence on society by providing the impetus for developing creative and compelling assessments that challenge those that can only survive due to their connections to officialdom.

Considering this matter from a balanced epistemological orientation presents us with an alternative way of thinking about the place of the social scientist in public affairs. It involves understanding the basic premise that each of these two approaches has some value, but that it is important to not confuse one with the other. Engaging in one's work prescriptively can be influential to others and may bring about some degree of social change over time. It is crucial to understand, however, that this work fits squarely in the domain of politics and not in that of social science. While this approach may lead to newer ways of looking at the issues involved, it can also interfere with the development of broadly insightful analyses of these issues. When investigators operating in this fashion come across evidence that runs counter to their agenda, they are inclined to find ways to work around that evidence, reconfigure it, or even sweep it under the rug in order to prevent it from getting in the way of their overarching political goals. Abiding by the ethics of politics can, in this sense, have a limiting influence on the likelihood that researchers will expand their understanding on the topics they seek to address.

Research done from an ethics of science point of view seeks to expose all elements of the social reality one is studying—including those that may be out of sync with the personal political goals of the researchers involved. Engaging in research from within the ethics of science and its concomitant emphasis on forging a deeper understanding of social phenomena has the potential to shape the directions of society—perhaps even more so than its political counterpart. This is due to the capacity of social science to forge what are often harsh, empirically grounded, and revealing analyses and conclusions about the social world, exposing injustice, absurdities, and corruption in ways that cannot be ignored. In other words, telling people how to conceptualize a particular social issue in a given context may actually be less effective in bringing about the desired result than challenging them to think critically and independently by exposing provocative truths that confront the sensibilities of those who would otherwise do nothing.

At the other end of the spectrum, we encounter scholars who argue that operating in the domain of social science means refraining from taking a stand on political issues altogether. Those adopting this position may be so devoted to what they perceive to be the proper ethos of social science that they consider it their responsibility to refrain from espousing any ethical concerns whatsoever in their work. According to this logic, it is not appropriate for social scientists to venture into the territory of values and ethics, because doing so would likely interfere with the objectivity of their analyses. Members of this group practice social science according to the belief that thinking about the impact of their research on the outside world would diminish their ability to develop a truly representative portrayal of their subject matter. Their job, as they see it, is limited to the task of gathering factual information and sharing it with others in a dispassionate and value-free manner.

The shortsightedness of this perspective can be understood by reaffirming a central argument of this book—that social science is inescapably connected to values. Engaging in social research from a balanced epistemological orientation means being aware of the principles of social science—and this includes taking into consideration the potential consequences of one's work. Denying the presence of values in social science does not make them go away. Instead, it furthers the myth that true social science does not concern itself with the affairs of people. Allowing this misunderstanding to pervade one's research can lead to several problems, not the least of which is the possibility of opening a pathway for self-interested parties to use social science to their own advantage, which can have a detrimental influence on the lives of individuals, groups, and society as a whole. The goal is thus to operate within the domain of social science, and this includes remaining conscious of the ways one's work is connected to the everyday world.

Rather than seeking to define in advance what types of research can be considered constructive or destructive to people's lives, there is an ongoing need to collectively discuss the issues involved and develop a provisional set of standards to serve as a guide in this regard. The conclusions social scientists draw from these discussions are not absolute or permanent in any way, but are connected to the values and ethics they hold dear and are formed in relation to the realities in place in any given context. It is therefore crucial that they retain a focus on the potential of social science to shed new light on social realities—including an awareness of the consequences of their research on others. When approaching their work with these concerns in mind, social scientists can develop new ways to understand social phenomena and provide the insight needed to face the future in an enlightened manner.

CONCLUSION

The unique character of social scientific knowledge requires researchers to conduct their investigations with a clear understanding of the epistemological and ethical issues involved. It demands that they build empirically grounded and theoretically informed analyses in an effort to illuminate past and present realities. Doing so means developing a sense of their own presuppositions and addressing these as needed in order to expand their horizons and strengthen their analyses. It also means having confidence in the merit of their own ideas and being willing to assert these clearly, even though they may differ significantly from established thought.

Approaching social science on the basis of a balanced epistemological orientation means accepting its interpretive nature while also being aware of its capacity to help us understand the continually changing dynamics of everyday life. It means acknowledging the fact that all social scientific conclusions are formed in relation to a particular set of culturally normative perspectives and are, nevertheless, quite capable of facilitating broad assessments of the social phenomena at hand. Social scientists do not assume that their ideas represent absolute truth, but make the strongest case possible for the analyses and conclusions they present. The primary intention of social research relying on a balanced epistemological orientation is to create illuminating analyses while also being cognizant of their potential fallibility.

Operating from a balanced epistemological orientation means asserting the validity of one's conceptual apparatus and taking a stand regarding what one considers to be the truth. Failure to do so can provide the opportunity for substandard analyses to fill the void, including those promulgated by individuals and institutions whose ideas are less insightful and less informed. The central goal of social research is much more than simply gathering factual information about the social world and sharing it with others. It involves participating in the effort to create new meanings about the issues and events taking place in people's personal lives. When social scientists engage in this work, they have already entered the ring, so to speak, where competing perspectives about the social world are being contested. In this sense, they are inescapably joining in the ongoing struggles to define social reality. Realizing this fundamental fact is the first step in doing high-quality, independent, insightful, and innovative social research. Adopting a balanced epistemological orientation in the endeavor of social science is a direct pathway to achieving this goal.

NOTES

1. In this section, I draw on the tripartite schema of Mills regarding the values of social science: truth, reason, and freedom. For a more in-depth elaboration of these three, please see: C. Wright Mills, *The Sociological Imagination* (Oxford: Oxford University Press, 1959).

2. Max Weber discusses the potential of social science to provide clarity in his essay: Max Weber, "Science as a Vocation," in *From Max Weber*, trans. Hans Gerth and C. Wright Mills (New York, NY: Oxford University Press, 1958; orig. pub. 1919). Mills points to reason as one of the central values of sociology in *The Sociological Imagination*.

3. This also builds on the work of C. Wright Mills in *The Sociological Imagination*.

4. Pierre Bourdieu discusses this idea in: Pierre Bourdieu and Loïc Wacquant, "From Ruling Class to Field of Power: An Interview with Pierre Bourdieu on La noblesse d'Etat," *Theory, Culture, and Society* 10 (1993): 19–44.

5. Bourdieu discusses the concept of reflexivity in the social sciences in a number of works. Please see: Bourdieu, "Vive la Crise!," 784.

6. Please see: Dorothy Smith, "Methods of Writing Patriarchy," ed. Ruth Wallace, *Feminism and Sociological Theory* (Newbury Park, CA: Sage, 1989), pp. 34–64.

7. Dorothy Smith, "Methods of Writing Patriarchy."

Bibliography

Adorno, Theodor. "Sociology and Empirical Research." In *The Positivist Dispute in German Sociology*, edited by T. W. Adorno, H. Albert, R. Dahrendorf, J. Habermas, H. Pilot, and K. R. Popper, 68–87. London: Heinemann, 1967.

Antonio, Robert. "The Origin, Development, and Contemporary Status of Critical Theory." *The Sociological Quarterly* 24, no. 3 (Summer 1983): 325–351.

Apel, Karl-Otto. "Regulative Ideas or Sense-Events? An Attempt to Determine the Logos of Hermeneutics." In *The Question of Hermeneutics: Essays in Honor of Joseph J. Kockelmans*, edited by Timothy J. Stapleton, 37–60. New York, NY: Springer, 1994.

Ayer, A. J., ed. *Logical Positivism*. New York, NY: The Free Press, 1959.

Babones, Salvatore. "Interpretive Quantitative Methods for the Social Sciences." *Sociology* 50, no. 3 (May 2015): 453–469.

Barber, Benjamin. "Three Scenarios for the Future of Technology and Strong Democracy." *Political Science Quarterly* 113, no. 4 (Winter 1998–1999): 573–589.

Benjamin, Walter. *Origin of the German Tragic Drama*. New York, NY: Verso, 2009.

Berger, Peter and Thomas Luckmann. *The Social Construction of Reality*. Garden City, NY: Doubleday and Company, 1967.

Bernstein, Richard. "From Hermeneutics to Praxis." *Review of Metaphysics* 35, no. 4 (June 1982): 823–845.

Bernstein, Richard. *The New Constellation: Ethical-Political Horizons of Modernity/Postmodernity*. Cambridge, MA: MIT Press, 1992.

Bernstein, Richard. *The Pragmatic Turn*. Cambridge, UK: Polity Press, 2010.

Blumer, Herbert. "Sociological Analysis and the Variable." *American Sociological Review* 21, no. 6 (December 1956): 683–690.

Blumer, Herbert. *Symbolic Interactionism*. Englewood Cliffs, NJ: Prentice-Hall, 1969.

Boas, Franz. "The Study of Geography." *Science* 9, no. 210 (February 1887): 137–141.

Boas, Franz. "The History of Anthropology." In *A Franz Boas Reader: The Shaping of American Anthropology, 1883–1911*, edited by George W. Stocking Jr., 23–35. Chicago, IL: University of Chicago Press, 1974.

Boas, Franz. *Race, Language, and Culture*. New York, NY: The Macmillan Company, 1940.

Boas, Franz. *The Mind of Primitive Man*. New York, NY: Macmillan Co., 1944.

Boas, Franz. *Anthropology and Modern Life*. New York, NY: Dover, 1986.

Bourdieu, Pierre and Jean-Claude Passeron. *Reproduction in Education, Society, and Culture*. New York, NY: Sage, 1977.

Bourdieu, Pierre. *Distinction: A Social Critique of the Judgement of Taste*. London, UK: Routledge, 2010.

Bourdieu, Pierre. "Vive la Crise! For Heterodoxy in Social Science." *Theory and Society* 17, no. 5 (September 1988): 773–787.

Bourdieu, Pierre, J. C. Chamboredon, and J. C. Passeron. *The Craft of Sociology: Epistemological Preliminaries*. Berlin and New York, NY: Walter de Gruyter, 1991.

Bourdieu, Pierre. "Thinking About Limits." *Theory, Culture, & Society* 9, no. 1 (February 1992): 37–49.

Bourdieu, Pierre and Loïc Wacquant. "From Ruling Class to Field of Power: An Interview with Pierre Bourdieu on La Noblesse d'Etat." *Theory, Culture, and Society* 10, no. 3 (August 1993): 19–44.

Brent, Joseph. *Charles Sanders Peirce: A Life*. Bloomington, IN: Indiana University Press, 1998.

Brown, Donald. *Human Universals*. New York, NY: McGraw-Hill, 1991.

Brown, Michael. "Cultural Relativism (2.0)." *Current Anthropology* 49, no. 3 (June 2008): 363–383.

Bryant, Christopher G. A. *Positivism in Social Theory and Research*. New York, NY: St. Martin's Press, 1985.

Bulmer, Martin. *The Chicago School of Sociology: Institutionalization, Diversity, and the Rise of Sociological Research*. Chicago, IL: University of Chicago Press, 1984.

Charmaz, Kathy. *Constructing Grounded Theory*. New York, NY: Sage, 2014.

Cicourel, Aaron. *Method and Measurement in Sociology*. New York, NY: Free Press, 1964.

Cicourel, Aaron. "I am NOT Opposed to Quantification or Formalization or Modeling, But Do Not Want to Pursue Quantitative Methods That Are Not Commensurate With the Research Phenomena Addressed. Aaron Cicourel in Conversation With Andreas Witzel and Günter Mey." *Forum: Qualitative Social Research* 5, no. 3 (September 2004): article 41.

Comte, Auguste. "Plan of the Scientific Operations Necessary for Reorganizing Society." In *On Intellectuals*, edited by Philip Rieff, 248–251. Garden City, NY: Doubleday & Co. Publishers, 1969.

Comte, Auguste. "The Positive Philosophy." In *Man and the Universe: The Philosophers of Science*, edited by Saxe Commins and Robert N. Linscott, 213–237. New York, NY: Random House, 1947.

Comte, Auguste. *System of Positive Polity*. London: Longmans, Green, and Co., 1875.

Comte, Auguste. *The Positive Philosophy of Auguste Comte*, edited and translated by Harriet Martineau. London: George Bell & Sons, 1896.

Connolly, William E. *Politics and Ambiguity*. Madison, WI: University of Wisconsin Press, 1987.

Derrida, Jacques. *Of Grammatology*, translated by Gayatri Chakravorty Spivak. Paris: Les Editions de Minuit, 1967.

Derrida, Jacques. *Writing and Difference*, translated by Alan Bass. Chicago, IL: University of Chicago Press, 1978.

Derrida, Jacques. *Positions*, translated by Alan Bass. Chicago, IL: University of Chicago Press, 1981.

Dewey, John. *The Public and Its Problems*. Chicago, IL: Swallow, 1954.

Dilthey, Wilhelm. *Selected Works: Volume III: The Formation of the Historical World in the Human Sciences*, edited by Rudolf A. Makkreel and Frithjof Rodi. Princeton, NJ: Princeton University Press, 2002.

Dilthey, Wilhelm. *Descriptive Psychology and Historical Understanding*, translated by Richard M. Zaner and Kenneth L. Heiges. The Hague: Martinus Nuhoff, 1977.

DuBois, W. E. B. *The Social Theory of W.E.B. DuBois*. New York, NY: Sage, 2004.

Foucault, Michel. *The Order of Things: An Archaeology of the Human Sciences*. London: Routledge, 2005.

Foucault, Michel. *The History of Sexuality Volume 1: An Introduction*, translated by Robert Hurley. New York, NY: Pantheon Books, 1978.

Foucault, Michel. *Power/Knowledge: Selected Interviews and Other Writings 1972–1977*, edited by Colin Gordon. New York, NY: Pantheon Books, 1972.

Foucault, Michel. *Discipline and Punish: The Birth of the Prison*. New York, NY: Random House, 1979.

Foucault, Michel. "What is Enlightenment?" In *The Foucault Reader*, edited by Paul Rabinow, 32–50. New York, NY: Pantheon Books, 1984.

Gadamer, Hans-Georg. *Truth and Method*. New York, NY: Continuum, 1977.

Gadamer, Hans-Georg. *Gadamer on Celan: "Who Am I and Who Are You?" and Other Essays*, edited and translated by Richard Heinemann and Bruce Krajewski. Albany, NY: SUNY Press, 1997.

Gadamer, Hans-Georg. *Reason in the Age of Science*. Cambridge, MA: MIT Press, 1981.

Gadamer, Hans-Georg. *Language and Linguisticality in Gadamer's Hermeneutics*, edited by Lawrence K. Schmidt. New York, NY: Lexington Books, 2000.

Gadamer, Hans-Georg. *The Beginning of Knowledge*, translated by Rod Coltman. New York, NY: Continuum, 2002.

Garfinkel, Harold. *Ethnomethodology*. Englewood Cliffs, NJ: Prentice-Hall, 1967.

Garfinkel, Harold. "Principal Theoretical Notions." In *Seeing Sociologically: The Routine Grounds of Social Action*, edited by A. W. Rawls, 101–205. Boulder, CO and London: Paradigm Publishers, 2006.

Gattone, Charles. *The Social Scientist as Public Intellectual: Critical Reflections in a Changing World*. Lanham, MD: Rowman & Littlefield, 2006.

Geertz, Clifford. *The Interpretation of Cultures*. New York, NY: Basic Books, 1973.

Gellner, Ernest. *Relativism and the Social Sciences*. Cambridge: Cambridge University Press, 1985.

Giddens, Anthony, ed. *Positivism and Sociology*. Portsmouth, New Hampshire: Heinemann, 1974.

Glaser, Barney and Anselm Strauss. *The Discovery of Grounded Theory: Strategies for Qualitative Research*. Chicago, IL: Aldine, 1967.

Goffman, Erving. *Frame Analysis: An Essay on the Organization of Experience*. Boston, MA: Northeastern University Press, 1974.

Grondin, Jean. *Introduction to Philosophical Hermeneutics*. New Haven, CT: Yale University Press, 1994.

Guba, Egon and Yvonna Lincoln. "Competing Paradigms in Qualitative Research." In *Handbook of Qualitative Research*, edited by Norman Denzin and Yvonna Lincoln, 105–117. New York, NY: Sage, 1994.

Habermas, Jürgen. *The Structural Transformation of the Public Sphere: An Inquiry Into a Category of Bourgeois Society*, translated by Thomas Burger. Cambridge, MA: The MIT Press, 1991.

Habermas, Jürgen. *Knowledge and Human Interests*, translated by Jeremy Shapiro. Boston, MA: Beacon, 1971.

Habermas, Jürgen. "Discussion on Value-Freedom and Objectivity." In *Max Weber and Sociology Today*, edited by Otto Stammer, translated by Kathleen Morris, 78–82. New York, NY: Harper and Row, 1971.

Habermas, Jürgen. *Theory and Practice*. Boston, MA: Beacon, 1973.

Habermas, Jürgen. *Habermas: Critical Debates*, edited by John B. Thompson and David Held. London: MacMillan, 1982.

Habermas, Jürgen. *The Theory of Communicative Action: Reason and the Rationalization of Society, Volume 1*, translated by Thomas McCarthy. Boston, MA: Beacon, 1985.

Habermas, Jürgen. *The Theory of Communicative Action: Lifeworld and System: A Critique of Functionalist Reason, Volume 2*, translated by Thomas McCarthy. Boston, MA: Beacon, 1985.

Habermas, Jürgen. "The Entwinement of Myth and Enlightenment: Rereading *Dialectic of Enlightenment*." *New German Critique* 26, no. 26 (Summer 1982): 13–30.

Habermas, Jürgen. "Modernity – An Incomplete Project." In *The Anti-Aesthetic: Essays on Postmodern Culture*, edited by Hal Foster, 3–16. Port Townsend, WA: Bay Press, 1983.

Habermas, Jürgen. "The Dualism of the Natural and Cultural Sciences." In *On the Logic of the Social Sciences*, 1–43. Cambridge, MA: MIT Press, 1988.

Habermas, Jürgen. *The Philosophical Discourse of Modernity*, translated by Frederick G. Lawrence. Cambridge, MA: MIT Press, 1992.

Heidegger, Martin. *Being and Time*. New York, NY: Harper & Row, 1962.

Heidegger, Martin. *Discourse on Thinking*. New York, NY: Harper & Row, 1966.

Horkheimer, Max. *Eclipse of Reason*. New York, NY: Continuum, 1974.

Horkheimer, Max and Theodor Adorno. *Dialectic of Enlightenment*, translated by John Cumming. New York, NY: Continuum, 1993.

Husserl, Edmund. *Logical Investigations, Volume 1*. Milton Park: Routledge, 2008.

Husserl, Edmund. *Logical Investigations, Volume 2*. Milton Park: Routledge, 2006.

Husserl, Edmund. *Ideas Pertaining to a Pure Phenomenology and to a Phenomenological Philosophy – First Book: General Introduction to a Pure Phenomenology*, translated by F. Kersten. The Hague: Martinus Nijhoff, 1982.

Husserl, Edmund. *Ideas Pertaining to a Pure Phenomenology and to a Phenomenological Philosophy – Second Book: Studies in the Phenomenology of Constitution*, translated by Richard Rojcewicz and André Schuwer. Dordrecht: Kluwer, 2000.

Husserl, Edmund. *Cartesian Meditations*, translated by J. S. Churchill and K. Ameriks. London, UK: Routledge, 1973.

Husserl, Edmund. *The Crisis of European Sciences and Transcendental Phenomenology*, translated by David Carr. Evanston, IL: Northwestern University Press, 1970.

Husserl, Edmund. *The Essential Husserl: Basic Writings in Transcendental Phenomenology*, edited by Donn Welton. Bloomington, IN: Indiana University Press, 1999.

James, William. *The Will to Believe*. Adelaide, Australia: University of Adelaide Press, 2014.

James, William. "Philosophical Conceptions and Practical Results." *University Chronicle* 1, no. 4 (September 1898): 287–310.

James, William. *Pragmatism: A New Name for Some Old Ways of Thinking*. Adelaide, Australia: University of Adelaide Press, 2014.

James, William. *The Meaning of Truth: A Sequel to 'Pragmatism.'* Adelaide, Australia: University of Adelaide Press, 2014.

Jameson, Fredric. "Postmodernism and Consumer Society." In *The Cultural Turn: Selected Writings on the Postmodern, 1983–1998*, 1–21. New York, NY: Verso, 1998.

Kuhn, Thomas. *The Structure of Scientific Revolutions*. Chicago, IL: University of Chicago Press, 1970.

Lyotard, Jean-François. *The Differend: Phrases in Dispute*, translated by George Van Den Abbeele. Minneapolis, MN: University of Minnesota Press, 1983.

Lyotard, Jean-François. *The Postmodern Condition: A Report on Knowledge*, translated by Geoff Bennington and Brian Massumi. Minneapolis, MN: University of Minnesota Press, 1988.

Malinowski, Bronislaw. *A Diary in the Strict Sense of the Term*. New York, NY: Harcourt, Brace & World, 1967.

Mannheim, Karl. "The Sociology of Intellectuals." *Theory, Culture, & Society* 10, no. 3 (August 1993): 69–80.

Mannheim, Karl. *Ideology and Utopia: An Introduction to the Sociology of Knowledge*. New York, NY: Harcourt, Brace, & World, 1968.

Margolis, Joseph. *The Truth About Relativism*. Oxford, UK: Blackwell, 1991.

Marinopoulou, Anastasia. *Critical Theory and Epistemology: The Politics of Modern Thought and Science*. Manchester: Manchester University Press, 2017.

Mayhall, C. Wayne. *On Logical Positivism*. Belmont, CA: Wadsworth, 2003.

Merleau-Ponty, Maurice. *Phenomenology of Perception*. London, UK: Routledge, 2002.

Mills, C. Wright. *The Sociological Imagination*. Oxford: Oxford University Press, 1959.

Miller, James. *The Passion of Michel Foucault*. New York, NY: Simon & Schuster Press, 1993.

Neurath, Otto, J. Hahn, and R. Carnap. "The Scientific Conception of the World: The Vienna Circle." In *Empiricism and Sociology*, edited by M. Neurath and R. S. Cohen, 299–318. Dordrecht: Reidel, 1973.

Nietzsche, Friedrich. *The Birth of Tragedy*, translated by Walter Kaufman. New York, NY: Vintage Books, 1967.

Nietzsche, Friedrich. *The Genealogy of Morals*, edited by Dr. Oscar Levy, translated by Horace B. Samuel and J. M. Kennedy. Edinburgh and London: T. N. Foulis, 1913.

Nietzsche, Friedrich. *Beyond Good and Evil: Prelude to a Philosophy of the Future*, translated by Walter Kaufmann. New York, NY: Vintage Books, 1989.

Nietzsche, Friedrich. *The Will to Power*, edited by Walter Kaufmann, translated by Walter Kaufmann and R. J. Hollingdale. New York, NY: Vintage, 1967.

Nietzsche, Friedrich. *Ecce Homo: How One Becomes What One Is*, translated by Walter Kaufman. New York, NY: Vintage Books, 1969.

Oevermann, Ulrich, Tilman Allert, Elisabeth Konau, and Jürgen Krambeck. "Structures of Meaning and Objective Hermeneutics." In *Modern German Sociology, European Perspectives: A Series in Social Thought and Cultural Criticism*, edited by Volker Meja, Dieter Misgeld, and Nico Stehr, 436–447. New York, NY: Columbia University Press, 1987.

Peirce, Charles Sanders. *The Essential Peirce, Volume 1*, edited by N. Houser and C. Kloesel. Bloomington, IN: Indiana University Press, 1992.

Peirce, Charles Sanders. *Collected Papers of Charles Sanders Peirce, Volumes 1–6*, edited by Charles Hartshorne and Paul Weiss. Cambridge, MA: Harvard University Press, 1931–1935.

Peirce, Charles Sanders. *Collected Papers of Charles Sanders Peirce, Volumes 7–8*, edited by Arthur W. Burks. Cambridge, MA: Harvard University Press, 1958.

Perry, Ralph Barton. *The Thought and Character of William James*. Nashville, TN: Vanderbilt University Press, 1996.

Polanyi, Michael and Harry Prosch. *Meaning*. Chicago, IL: University of Chicago Press, 1996.

Popper, Karl. "The Logic of the Social Sciences." In *The Positivist Dispute in German Sociology*, edited by T. W. Adorno, H. Albert, R. Dahrendorf, J. Habermas, H. Pilot, and K. R. Popper, translated by Glyn Adey and David Frisby, 87–104. London: Heinemann, 1977.

Rabinow, Paul. *Interpretive Social Science: A Second Look*. Berkeley, CA: University of California Press, 1987.

Richardson, Frank and Blaine Fowers. "Interpretive Social Science: An Overview." *American Behavioral Scientist* 41, no. 4 (January 1998): 465–495.

Ricoeur, Paul. *The Philosophy of Paul Ricoeur*. Boston, MA: Beacon, 1978.

Ricoeur, Paul. *Hermeneutics and the Human Sciences: Essays on Language, Action, and Interpretation*, edited and translated by John B. Thompson. Cambridge: Cambridge University Press, 1981.

Ricoeur, Paul. *Oneself As Another*. Chicago, IL: University of Chicago Press, 1992.

Rorty, Richard. *Philosophy and the Mirror of Nature*. Princeton, NJ: Princeton University Press, 1979.

Rorty, Richard. *Contingency, Irony, and Solidarity*. Cambridge: Cambridge University Press, 1989.

Rorty, Richard. *Philosophy and Social Hope*. New York, NY: Penguin, 2000.

Schütz, Alfred. "Common-Sense and Scientific Interpretation of Human Action." *Philosophy and Phenomenological Research* 14, no. 1 (September 1953): 1–38.

Schütz, Alfred. "The Social World and the Theory of Social Action." *Social Research* 27, no. 2 (Summer, 1960): 203–221.

Schütz, Alfred. "On Multiple Realities." In *Collected Papers: Studies in Social Theory*, 207–259. The Hague: Martinus Nijhoff, 1962.

Schütz, Alfred. *The Phenomenology of the Social World*. Evanston, IL: Northwestern University Press, 1967.

Schütz, Alfred. *Alfred Schütz: Collected Papers II, Studies in Social Theory*, edited by Arvid Brodersen. The Hague: Martinus Nijhoff, 1976.

Smart, Barry. *Michel Foucault*. New York, NY: Tavistock Publications, 1985.

Smith, David Woodruff. *Husserl*. London, UK: Routledge, 2007.

Smith, Dorothy. "Methods of Writing Patriarchy," In *Feminism and Sociological Theory*, edited by Ruth Wallace, 34–64. Newbury Park, CA: Sage, 1989.

Sproule, Michael. "Propaganda Studies in American Social Science: The Rise and Fall of the Critical Paradigm." *Quarterly Journal of Speech* 73, no. 1 (February 1987): 60–78.

Stadler, Friedrich. *The Vienna Circle: Studies in the Origins, Development, and Influence of Logical Empiricism*. New York, NY: Springer, 2015.

Steinmetz, George, ed. *The Politics of Method in the Human Sciences: Positivism and Its Epistemological Others*. Durham, NC: Duke University Press, 2005.

Stryker, Sheldon. *Symbolic Interactionism*. Caldwell, NJ: Blackburn Press, 2003.

Taylor, Charles. *Philosophy and the Human Sciences: Philosophical Papers, Volume 2*. Cambridge, UK: Cambridge University Press, 1985.

Thomassen, Lasse. *Deconstructing Habermas*. London, UK: Routledge, 2008.

Turner, Jonathan H. "In Defense of Positivism." *Sociological Theory* 3, no. 2 (Autumn 1985): 24–30.

Veblen, Thorstein. *The Higher Learning in America*. New Brunswick, NJ: Transaction, 1993.

Weber, Max. *The Methodology of the Social Sciences*, edited and translated by Edward Shils and Henry Finch. New York, NY: Free Press, 1949.

Weber, Max. *The Protestant Ethic and the Spirit of Capitalism*, translated by Talcott Parsons. New York, NY: Charles Scribner's Sons, 1958.

Weber, Max. *From Max Weber: Essays in Sociology*, translated by Hans Gerth and C. Wright Mills. New York, NY: Oxford University Press, 1958.

Weber, Max. *Economy and Society: An Outline of Interpretive Sociology*, translated by Guenther Roth and Claus Wittich. Berkeley, CA: University of California Press, 1978.

Weber, Max. *The Theory of Social and Economic Organization*, translated by A. M. Henderson and Talcott Parsons. New York, NY: Oxford University Press, 1947.

Williams, Michael. *Problems of Knowledge: A Critical Introduction to Epistemology*. Oxford: Oxford University Press, 2001.

Winch, Peter. *The Idea of a Social Science and Its Relation to Philosophy*. London, UK: Routledge, 1958.

Wittgenstein, Ludwig. *Philosophical Investigations*. Englewood Cliffs, NJ: Prentice-Hall, 1958.

Zimmerman, Jens. *Hermeneutics: A Very Short Introduction*. Oxford: Oxford University Press, 2015.

Index

About the Author

Charles F. Gattone is associate professor of sociology at the University of Florida. He is the author of the book *The Social Scientist As Public Intellectual: Critical Reflections in a Changing World* and the articles "The Social Scientist as Public Intellectual in an Age of Mass Media," "Image and Persuasion: The Machiavellian World of Advertising and Public Relations," "The Role of the Intellectual in Public Affairs," and "Media and Politics in the Information Age."

www.ingramcontent.com/pod-product-compliance
Lightning Source LLC
Chambersburg PA
CBHW022325280326
41932CB00010B/1226